Mind Engineered

The Rise of the External Mind in the Age of AI

Moawiah Naffaa, PhD

Copyright and Disclaimer

Mind Engineered explores how artificial intelligence is reshaping human thinking, learning, memory, judgment, creativity, and cognition. The book develops a conceptual framework for understanding the emerging relationship between human minds and intelligent systems and considers its broader implications for individuals, education, culture, and society.

The perspectives and frameworks presented in this book reflect the author's synthesis and interpretation of a rapidly developing technological and cognitive landscape. As artificial intelligence continues to evolve, new research, technologies, and human experiences will continue to expand and refine our understanding of this relationship.

At the center of the book is the concept of the **External Mind**—a framework for examining how aspects of memory, reasoning, imagination, learning, and decision-making increasingly unfold through interaction between human cognition and intelligent systems. The concepts developed throughout *Mind Engineered* are offered as a foundation for understanding and engaging with this emerging cognitive transformation.

Readers are encouraged to approach artificial intelligence with curiosity, discernment, and independent judgment, recognizing that the value of any intelligent system ultimately depends on how thoughtfully it is understood and used.

Mind Engineered, the **External Mind** framework, and the related concepts developed throughout this work represent the author's original intellectual formulation and interpretation of the evolving relationship between human cognition and artificial intelligence.

Published by
Moawiah Naffaa, PhD

Permissions and inquiries
Moawiah.Naffaa@proton.me

Table of Contents

Preface

This book was not planned.

It emerged from a quiet realization that grew impossible to ignore: I was no longer thinking alone.

Like many people, I began using AI as a tool—for drafting, exploring ideas, testing arguments, asking questions. But over time, something subtle shifted. The interaction no longer felt like using software. It felt like thinking with something. Dialogues with a machine began to resemble dialogues with my own mind. Questions led to reflections I had not anticipated. Explanations helped me understand my own thoughts more clearly. Ideas evolved not in isolation, but in exchange.

What I was experiencing did not fit the familiar categories of "technology use," "productivity," or even "creativity." It felt cognitive. Structural. Foundational.

It felt as though part of the thinking process had moved outside the boundaries of my brain.

This book grew from that realization.

In *Creativity Engineered*, I explored how humans create with AI. I examined how artificial intelligence can amplify imagination, support innovation, and reshape the creative process. But as that work concluded, a deeper question surfaced:

If AI can participate in **creativity**, what is it doing to **thinking itself**?

This question is not technological. It is human. It touches memory, learning, identity, perception, and the very nature of cognition. It asks not what AI can do, but what humans are becoming as AI becomes a permanent cognitive companion.

We are witnessing a shift that is easy to miss because it happens quietly, daily, and without spectacle. There are no dramatic announcements marking this change. No visible revolution. Yet millions of people now think, learn, plan, imagine, and decide in dialogue with artificial systems. The mind is no longer confined to the biological brain. It is extending into digital space.

This book is an attempt to understand that **extension**.

It is not a guide to tools, prompts, or productivity. It is not a forecast of distant futures. It is an exploration of a transformation already underway—one that reshapes how we think, remember, imagine, and know.

This book is not about what AI can do.
It is about what AI is already doing to the structure of human thinking.

If *Creativity Engineered* was about how we create with AI, *Mind Engineered* is about how we think with AI.

Together, these books form an unfolding exploration of how artificial intelligence is reshaping the architecture of the human mind — from creativity, to cognition, to identity, and beyond.

And what that means for the future of being **human**.

The External Mind Loop

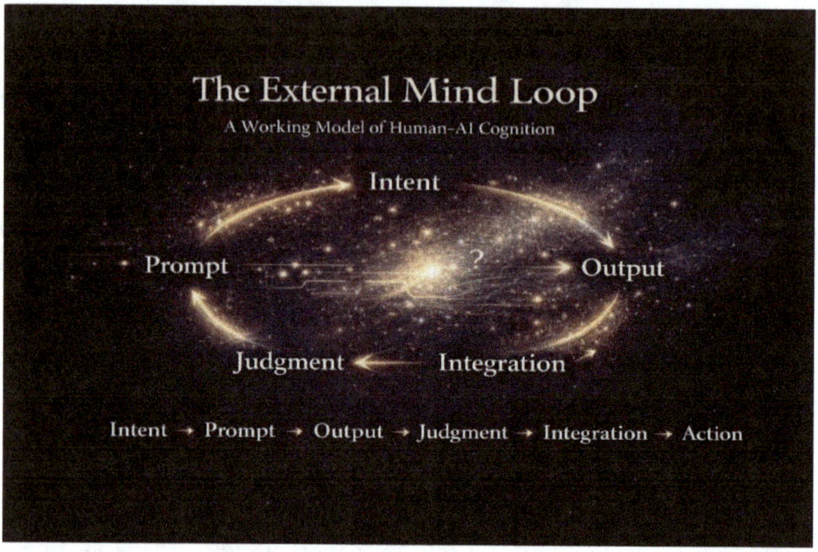

A Working Model of Human–AI Cognition

When humans think with artificial intelligence, cognition does not unfold randomly.
It follows a repeatable structure.

This structure can be described as a loop—one in which intention becomes dialogue, dialogue becomes output, and output reshapes thought and action. This loop defines how the **External Mind** operates in practice.

The External Mind Loop

Intent → Prompt → Output → Judgment → Integration → Action

This is not a productivity sequence.
It is a cognitive architecture.

Intent

Every interaction begins with intent, whether conscious or implicit.
Intent defines *why* the mind engages: curiosity, confusion, creativity, verification, planning, or reflection.

Weak intent produces shallow cognition.
Clear intent shapes the entire loop.

Prompt

The **prompt** is intent translated into language.

This is the moment when internal thought leaves the brain and becomes external. Prompting is not a technical step; it is a cognitive act that forces vague intuition into structured inquiry.

The quality of the prompt reflects the clarity of thought at this stage.

Output

The output is the system's response: explanation, synthesis, reframing, or simulation.

Output is not truth.
It is **raw cognitive material**.

Its value depends entirely on what follows.

Judgment

Judgment is the critical human function in the loop.

Here, the thinker evaluates the output:

- Is it accurate?
- Is it coherent?
- Is it relevant?
- Is it misleading or incomplete?

Judgment cannot be automated.
This is where intelligence resides.

Integration

Integration occurs when evaluated output is absorbed into the thinker's internal model.

This may involve revising assumptions, connecting ideas, refining understanding, or reshaping future questions. Integration is where learning actually happens.

Without integration, interaction remains superficial.

Action

Action is where cognition leaves the loop and enters the world.

This may take the form of writing, deciding, designing, teaching, or changing perspective. Action often generates new intent, restarting the loop.

The External Mind is therefore **recursive**, not linear.

Failure Modes

The loop breaks down when cognition is bypassed:

- **Hallucination acceptance** — treating output as fact
- **Over-trust** — outsourcing judgment
- **Dependency** — prompting without intent
- **Shallow prompting** — vague inputs that prevent insight

These are not system failures.
They are cognitive failures.

Skill Upgrades

The power of the External Mind depends on the human side of the loop:

- **Higher-quality questions**
- **Active verification**
- **Reflective pauses**
- **Boundary-setting**

Mastery lies not in using AI more—but in using it deliberately.

The Architecture of Thinking with AI

Two people can use the same AI system and produce radically different outcomes.

The difference is not access.
It is **intent, judgment, and integration**.

The **External Mind Loop** is the basic unit of thinking with machines.
It will reappear throughout this book—in memory, learning, creativity, and identity—because it explains *how* cognition now unfolds.

Once you see the loop, you cannot unsee it.

Introduction — When Thinking Left the Brain

For most of human history, thinking was assumed to occur in one place: inside the head.

The brain was considered the sole container of memory, reasoning, imagination, and decision-making. Books stored information, but thinking remained internal. Tools helped us act, but they did not participate in cognition. Even the internet, vast as it became, was largely treated as a repository of information rather than an active partner in thought.

That assumption is no longer true.

Today, millions of people sit down to think and begin not by closing their eyes, but by opening a conversation with AI. They ask questions, explore ideas, test arguments, clarify confusion, and generate possibilities through dialogue. They do not merely retrieve information; they develop thoughts in real time with a system that responds, adapts, and elaborates.

Thinking is no longer a solitary neurological process. It has become distributed across brain and machine.

This shift is subtle, but profound. It represents a cognitive reorganization unlike any before it. Writing externalized memory. Printing democratized knowledge. The internet globalized access to information. But AI does something different: it participates in the formation of thought itself.

When you brainstorm with AI, your ideas do not emerge solely from internal reflection. They evolve through interaction. When you learn with AI, understanding is not constructed only through reading and memorization, but through dynamic exchange. When you plan, design, or reflect with AI, the boundaries between internal cognition and external assistance blur.

This is the birth of what can be called the **External Mind**.

The **External Mind** is not a metaphor. It is a functional reality in which part of the cognitive process occurs outside the biological brain, in continuous interaction with intelligent systems. Memory, imagination, problem-solving, and decision-making increasingly unfold across this hybrid space.

Yet most people experiencing this shift do not have a language for it. They feel that thinking is changing, but cannot articulate how. They notice they remember less but understand more. They sense that ideas come faster, but do not know why. They feel intellectually supported, but cannot explain the mechanism.

This book provides that **language**.

It examines how AI is reshaping memory, learning, imagination, intelligence, identity, and culture—not in theory, but in everyday cognitive life.

We are not entering an age where machines think **for** us.

We are entering an age where humans think **with** machines.

Understanding this shift is essential, because it is already redefining what it means to think at all.

The External Mind names a condition in which cognition unfolds across brain and interactive system rather than within the brain alone.

When I say the External Mind is not a metaphor, I do not mean that consciousness lives inside machines or that identity migrates into code.

The claim is structural, not mystical.

The External Mind describes a functional shift in how cognition unfolds in practice. It names a condition in which reasoning, memory reconstruction, idea formation, and reflection increasingly occur through interaction with intelligent systems.

This is not a claim about where the self-resides. It is a claim about where cognitive work now happens.

The mind remains human. But its operational field has expanded.

Part I — The End of the Isolated Mind

This part establishes a foundational correction.
It reframes the mind not as an isolated biological unit, but as a system that has always relied on external structures to think. The focus here is not on AI itself, but on understanding why the idea of a fully internal mind was always incomplete.

But this view, while intuitive, has never been entirely true.

Even before the age of AI, humans have always relied on external structures to think. We wrote things down to remember. We drew diagrams to understand. We used maps to navigate. We built libraries to extend knowledge beyond individual memory. We developed language itself as a shared cognitive system. Thinking has never been purely internal—it has always been supported, shaped, and extended by tools outside the brain.

What is changing now is not the existence of external support for thought, but its nature.

For the first time in history, the external structure we use is not passive. It does not simply store information. It responds, engages, generates, and participates in the thinking process. AI is not a notebook. It is not a book. It is not a search engine. It is an interactive system that enters into dialogue with our thoughts.

This is where the idea of the **isolated mind** begins to break down.

This shift is subtle because it feels natural. We experience it as convenience, assistance, or efficiency. But beneath that surface lies a profound transformation: the boundaries of cognition are expanding.

This part of the book lays the foundation for understanding that transformation.

We will begin by revisiting a forgotten truth: the brain was never alone. We will trace how writing, books, tools, and the internet gradually externalized parts of human thought. We will then examine how AI crosses a critical threshold—moving from external support to active cognitive participation. And finally, we will see why this change is not merely technological, but a genuine cognitive revolution in how humans think.

Before we can understand the **External Mind**, we must first understand why the idea of the isolated mind was always incomplete.

1. The Brain Was Never Alone

We are taught from an early age that **thinking** happens inside the **brain**.

We imagine thoughts forming within the skull, memories stored in neural tissue, ideas generated through internal reflection. Intelligence is measured by what a person can recall without assistance. Learning is judged by what remains inside the mind when all external aids are removed.

This view feels obvious. Natural. Undeniable.

And yet, it has never been entirely true.

Long before the arrival of AI, humans have always relied on external structures to think. We write notes not only to remember, but to understand. We draw diagrams not only to show, but to reason. We use maps not only to navigate space, but to organize thought. We speak language not only to communicate, but to shape ideas. We build libraries, tools, symbols, and systems that extend our mental capacity beyond the limits of biological memory.

Thinking has always relied on structures beyond the brain. It has always been supported by the world around us.

What we often mistake as "internal thought" is, in reality, a continuous interaction between the brain and its external supports. The notebook on the desk, the sketch on the page, the words spoken aloud, the books on a shelf—these have always been part of the thinking process.

But we did not notice.

We did not notice because these external aids were passive. They stored information, but they did not respond. They helped us think, but they did not appear to participate in thinking. The cognitive center still felt internal, even though it was quietly extended into the environment.

This is why the idea of the **isolated mind** survived for so long.

This section begins by uncovering that hidden history. Before we can understand how AI is changing thinking, we must first recognize a deeper truth:

1.1 The Hidden History of External Thinking

Long before AI, long before computers, and even long before books, humans were already thinking with the world around them.

When early humans began making marks on stone, clay, and papyrus, they were not simply recording information. They were extending memory beyond the limits of the brain. Writing allowed thoughts to exist outside the mind, to be revisited, rearranged, and refined. A written note is not just a reminder; it is a continuation of thinking in physical form.

The same is true of drawing. Diagrams, sketches, and symbols are not decorations of thought; they are instruments of thought. Engineers sketch to understand structure. Mathematicians draw to see relationships. Artists draft to discover form. The act of placing ideas on a surface allows the mind to manipulate them in ways that would be impossible to hold internally.

Consider maps. A map does not merely show geography; it allows the mind to reason spatially across distances that cannot be mentally visualized all at once. Or consider diagrams and charts. These are not passive images. They organize complexity into patterns the brain can interact with. A scientist mapping a system, a student outlining notes, a thinker drawing connections between ideas—these are all forms of thinking distributed across brain and environment.

Even books serve this role. We often think of books as sources of information, but they are also cognitive extensions. When we read, underline, annotate, and return to passages, we are not simply consuming knowledge. We are engaging in an externalized dialogue with ideas that would otherwise exceed our internal capacity to process them.

Language itself is a form of shared cognition. Words are not stored privately in individual minds; they exist as a collective system that allows thoughts to be shaped, refined, and understood across people. Speaking aloud often clarifies ideas because language externalizes thought, making it available for reflection.

And beyond these, humans have always used tools as cognitive scaffolding. Calculators extend numerical reasoning. Musical instruments extend auditory imagination. Measuring devices extend perception. These tools do not just help us act; they help us think.

Thinking has never been a purely internal neurological event. It has always been a partnership between the brain and its environment. The notebook, the diagram, the map, the written word, and the spoken language have long functioned as extensions of mental processing.

The brain has always relied on **external supports** to think.

1.2 Why We Never Noticed This

If humans have always thought with external supports, why do we still believe that thinking happens only inside the brain?

The answer lies in the nature of those supports.

They were **passive**.

A notebook does not answer back. A map does not adapt. A book does not respond to questions. These tools stored information, organized ideas, and made thinking easier, but they did not appear to participate in cognition. They waited for us. They did not engage with us.

Because of this, thinking still felt internal. The brain remained the active agent, while the external world appeared as a silent helper. We interacted with tools, but the tools did not interact with us.

This distinction shaped our perception. We saw external objects as aids to thinking, not as components of thinking. The cognitive process still seemed centered inside the head, even though parts of it were already unfolding outside.

There is also a deeper psychological reason. We experience thoughts as internal sensations—images, words, and reflections that feel private and contained. When we use a pen, read a page, or draw a diagram, we still experience the mental activity as originating within us. The external support fades into the background of awareness.

So the myth of the **isolated mind** persisted.

External thinking existed, but it never felt like thinking.

That is what changes with **AI**.

For the first time, the external support does not simply store or display information. It responds, adapts, and participates in real time. The boundary between internal cognition and external assistance becomes visible. Thinking begins to feel like an interaction rather than a solitary act.

2. From Writing to Internet to AI — The Evolution of External Thinking

The idea that thinking can extend beyond the brain did not appear suddenly with AI.

It has been unfolding quietly across human history.

What feels today like a dramatic cognitive shift is, in fact, the latest step in a long and largely unnoticed progression. Over centuries, humans have gradually moved parts of their mental processes into the world around them. First through symbols, then through systems, then through networks—and now through intelligent interaction.

This evolution did not happen all at once. It occurred in **stages**.

Each stage changed how humans relate to memory, knowledge, and ultimately thought itself. Each stage reduced the burden on the biological brain while increasing the role of external structures in the cognitive process. And with each transition, humans adapted so naturally that the shift became invisible.

We did not experience these changes as revolutions in thinking. We experienced them as conveniences, tools, or cultural progress. Yet, beneath the surface, something far more profound was happening: the gradual relocation of cognitive work from inside the brain to outside it.

Writing allowed thoughts to persist outside memory.
Books and networks allowed knowledge to exist beyond individual minds.
AI now allows thinking to occur through interaction.

Seen in this light, AI is not an isolated technological breakthrough. It is the third major phase in the historical evolution of external thinking.

To understand why AI represents a genuine cognitive turning point, we must first understand the path that led here.

2.1 Writing: The First External Memory

The invention of writing marked the first moment in history when human thought could exist outside the brain in a permanent form.

Before writing, memory was biological. Knowledge lived only in the mind, transmitted through speech, repetition, and ritual. To remember was to hold information internally. To forget was to lose it forever. Thinking and remembering were inseparable because both depended entirely on the brain's limited capacity.

Writing changed that relationship.

When humans began inscribing symbols onto surfaces, memory was no longer confined to neural tissue. Thoughts could be placed onto clay, stone, papyrus, and paper. They could be revisited, reorganized, corrected, and expanded. A written note did not merely preserve an idea; it allowed the mind to return to it as if the thought were still present.

This was revolutionary.

For the first time, humans no longer had to remember everything internally. They could rely on an external surface to hold part of their memory. This did not weaken thinking; it strengthened it. By freeing the brain from the burden of total recall, writing created space for reflection, comparison, and more complex reasoning.

Writing did something subtle but profound:

It allowed memory to become **external**.

This was the birth of recorded thinking. Thoughts were no longer fleeting internal events. They became stable objects in the world that the mind could interact with. A written page became a partner in memory, extending the cognitive process beyond the skull.

The first step toward external thinking was not about knowledge or intelligence. It was about memory leaving the brain.

2.2 Printing, Books, and the Internet: External Knowledge

If writing externalized memory, the next transformation externalized knowledge.

The invention of the printing press multiplied written thought beyond individual ownership. Books allowed ideas to travel across time and geography. Libraries gathered human knowledge into shared spaces. Information was no longer personal or local—it became collective and accessible.

This shift altered how humans related to knowledge itself.

Before widespread books, knowing something meant storing it internally. After books, knowing increasingly meant knowing where to find it. The burden on memory decreased further. The mind no longer needed to retain vast amounts of information; it needed to navigate external repositories of knowledge.

The arrival of the internet accelerated this change dramatically. Information became instantly searchable, globally available, and continuously updated. Search engines replaced memorization with access. Instead of recalling facts, humans learned to retrieve them.

A quiet cognitive transition occurred:

Humans stopped memorizing knowledge and started **accessing** it.

Knowledge was no longer something contained within individuals. It existed outside, distributed across books, servers, databases, and networks. The brain adapted by becoming better at locating, filtering, and interpreting external information rather than storing it.

This was the second phase of external thinking.

Information became external and universally accessible. The mind no longer had to be a warehouse of facts. It became a navigator of knowledge.

2.3 AI: External Cognition

Writing externalized memory.
Books and the internet externalized knowledge.
AI externalizes thinking itself.

AI is not simply a place where information is stored. It is not merely a database or search engine. It engages, responds, elaborates, and adapts in real time. For the first time in history, the external system we use does not only preserve knowledge—it participates in the formation of thought.

When you ask AI a question, you are not retrieving a stored answer. You are engaging in a dynamic exchange that shapes your thinking. Ideas evolve through interaction. Clarifications arise through dialogue. Possibilities expand through response.

This marks the third phase of external thinking: from storing thoughts, to accessing information, to interacting with a system that actively participates in cognition.

3. The Birth of the External Mind

Up to this point, we have seen that the brain was never truly isolated and that external thinking has evolved across history—from writing, to books, to the internet, and now to AI.

But something new has happened.

A threshold has been crossed.

For the first time, the external structure we rely on does not merely store information or provide access to knowledge. It engages with us in a way that begins to resemble part of the thinking process itself. The relationship between brain and tool has changed from assistance to interaction.

This is where a new concept becomes necessary.

We need a way to describe a form of thinking that no longer happens entirely inside the biological brain, but unfolds through continuous exchange with an intelligent system. We need language to explain a cognitive experience that millions of people are already living, but few can articulate.

That concept is the **External Mind**.

The **External Mind** is not a metaphor. It is a description of a new cognitive reality in which memory, reasoning, imagination, and learning increasingly occur across both brain and AI. It names the condition in which part of the thinking process exists outside the skull, in dynamic dialogue with a digital system.

This section introduces and defines that idea.

Because before we can understand how AI is reshaping memory, learning, identity, and intelligence, we must first recognize what has quietly come into existence:

A mind that is no longer contained within the brain alone.

3.1 When External Support Becomes Cognitive Participation

For thousands of years, humans have used tools to **assist** thinking.

A notebook helps us remember.
A diagram helps us understand.
A book helps us learn.
A search engine helps us find information.

But in all these cases, the tools remained outside the thinking process. They supported cognition, but they did not enter into it. The brain remained the active center, while the tool remained passive. We acted upon the tool; the tool did not act back upon our thoughts.

This is the line that **AI crosses**.

AI does not simply wait for us to retrieve information. It responds. It elaborates. It reformulates. It suggests. It questions. It adapts to the direction of our inquiry. The interaction is no longer one-sided.

Something subtle but profound happens in this exchange.

The external aid becomes part of the **cognitive loop**.

When you ask AI a question, your thinking does not stop and resume after you receive an answer. Your thinking evolves through the response. You refine your thoughts based on what you see. You explore new directions suggested by the system. You reconsider assumptions. The process becomes circular and interactive rather than linear and internal.

Thinking begins to resemble a **feedback system** between brain and AI.

Your idea influences the AI's response.
The AI's response influences your next thought.
That thought reshapes the next interaction.

This continuous loop is what distinguishes assistance from participation.

AI is no longer outside the thinking process.

AI is inside it.

3.2 Defining the External Mind

This new condition requires a name.

The term **External Mind** describes a cognitive reality in which part of the thinking process occurs outside the biological brain, in continuous interaction with an intelligent system.

The **External Mind** is a practical description of how millions of people now think every day.

When you use AI to brainstorm, your imagination flows across both you and the system.
When you use AI to learn, understanding develops through dialogue rather than memorization.
When you use AI to plan, reason, or write, parts of the cognitive work unfold externally.
When you rely on AI to recall, summarize, or organize information, memory becomes shared across brain and machine.

In each case, memory, imagination, reasoning, and learning no longer occur solely within the brain. They move across a hybrid space where biological cognition and digital interaction function together.

This is a structural change in how thinking happens.

The mind is no longer a closed biological system. It is becoming a distributed system spanning neural processes and digital intelligence.

The External Mind names this new structure.

It explains why thinking with AI feels different from using any tool before it. It explains why people experience greater clarity, faster idea generation, and deeper reflection when they interact with AI. It explains why cognition now feels collaborative rather than solitary.

It is now spread across biological and digital space.

And this realization sets the stage for understanding why this shift is not merely technological, but a true cognitive revolution.

With this structure defined, the implications now unfold across memory, learning, and intelligence.

4. Why This Is a Cognitive Revolution, Not a Technological One

Most people describe the rise of **AI** as a technological breakthrough.

They speak of faster systems, smarter algorithms, and more powerful machines. They debate tools, applications, risks, and possibilities. The conversation centers on what AI can do and how it will change industries, jobs, and daily life.

But this framing misses something far more profound.

The most significant change is not happening in machines.

It is happening in **humans**.

What we are witnessing is not simply the arrival of a new technology, but a reorganization of how thinking itself occurs. The boundaries of cognition are shifting. The relationship between brain, memory, knowledge, and reasoning is being redefined. The structure of the mind is quietly expanding beyond the limits it has held for millennia.

Because this shift is mediated through technology, we mistake it for technological progress. But the true transformation is cognitive. It affects how we remember, how we learn, how we reason, how we imagine, and ultimately how we understand intelligence itself.

This section examines why the rise of the **External Mind** must be understood not as an advance in tools, but as the beginning of a new era in human cognition.

A change not in what machines can do—

But in what it now means for humans to **think**.

4.1 Why We Are Mislabeling This as "AI Progress"

When people speak about the rise of AI, they almost always frame it as a story of technological advancement.

They talk about faster processors, smarter models, larger datasets, and more capable systems. Headlines focus on what AI can write, design, predict, or automate. The discussion revolves around innovation, disruption, and the future of industries.

But this focus on the machine hides the more important transformation.

Because while AI is improving, the deeper change is happening in **us**.

What is shifting is not only what machines can do, but how humans now think in relation to those machines. The daily cognitive experience of millions of people is being reshaped. Memory habits are changing. Learning patterns are changing. Problem-solving approaches are changing. Imagination itself is changing.

Yet we describe all of this as "AI progress."

This is a mislabeling.

By centering the story on technology, we overlook the fact that the real transformation is occurring in human cognition. We see AI as the actor and humans as the observers. In reality, humans are the ones adapting, reorganizing, and extending their thinking processes through interaction with AI.

The narrative should not be:

AI is becoming more intelligent.

The narrative should be:

Humans are beginning to think differently.

But because the change arrives through a technological medium, we attribute the shift to the machine rather than to the evolving structure of the mind.

The story is not primarily about AI.

It is about us.

4.2 The Redefinition of Thinking

For centuries, **thinking** was defined as an internal mental activity.

It meant reasoning silently, recalling information from memory, imagining possibilities within the mind, and making decisions through internal reflection. Cognition was assumed to be a closed process occurring entirely inside the brain.

That definition no longer fits reality.

When people sit down to think today, they often begin by opening a dialogue with AI. They do not rely solely on internal reflection. They develop ideas through interaction. They refine understanding through exchange. They explore possibilities by engaging with an external system that responds and elaborates.

Once thinking becomes **interactive**, our definition of cognition must change.

This requires a change in how we define cognition itself. If part of the reasoning process occurs through dialogue with AI, if memory retrieval happens externally, if imagination expands through interaction, then thinking can no longer be described as a solitary neurological event.

In practice, thinking now includes:

- Asking AI questions to clarify understanding
- Exploring ideas through back-and-forth dialogue
- Using AI to simulate possibilities and alternatives
- Relying on AI to organize, summarize, and restructure information

These are not peripheral aids to thinking. They are part of the thinking process.

The structure of thinking has changed.

What once occurred entirely within the brain now unfolds across brain and machine. The cognitive boundary has expanded, and with it, the meaning of what it means to think.

4.3 The Redefinition of Intelligence

For most of modern history, intelligence has been measured by what a person can hold and manipulate internally.

Exams test recall without assistance. IQ tests measure pattern recognition and reasoning within the boundaries of the individual brain. Expertise is judged by how much knowledge someone carries in memory and how quickly they can retrieve it.

This model made sense in a world where thinking was assumed to occur entirely inside the mind.

But in the age of the **External Mind**, this definition becomes incomplete.

Today, intelligence is no longer limited to what you know internally. It increasingly depends on how effectively you can think across brain and AI. The ability to ask the right questions, guide dialogue, interpret responses, and integrate external input into reasoning becomes more important than memorizing vast amounts of information.

A person who knows less but knows how to think with AI may outperform someone who relies solely on internal memory.

It is a shift in its structure.

Intelligence is becoming **distributed**.

Intelligence no longer lives only in the head.
It lives in the loop.

It now includes the capacity to navigate, collaborate, and reason within a hybrid cognitive system. The skill lies not only in internal recall, but in orchestrating interaction between personal understanding and external cognitive support.

In this context, traditional measures like IQ begin to lose relevance. They evaluate isolated cognition, while real-world thinking increasingly occurs in partnership with intelligent systems. The metrics of intelligence must evolve to reflect this new reality.

What matters is no longer only what you know.

What matters is how you think across systems.

4.4 The Beginning of a New Cognitive Era

When thinking changes, everything built upon thinking changes with it.

The rise of the **External Mind** does not affect only individual cognition. It begins to reshape the foundations of education, work, society, and the development of future humans.

In education, memorization loses priority while reasoning, questioning, and dialogue gain importance. Learning becomes less about storing information and more about interacting with knowledge dynamically.

In work, problem-solving shifts from individual expertise to collaborative cognition between humans and AI. Decision-making, design, and innovation increasingly occur through hybrid thinking processes.

In society, communication, creativity, and knowledge exchange evolve as people rely on shared cognitive systems rather than isolated mental effort. Cultural norms around intelligence, expertise, and productivity begin to transform.

And perhaps most significantly, children growing up with AI will never experience thinking as a purely internal activity. For them, interacting with an external cognitive partner will feel natural, not revolutionary.

This marks the beginning of a new epoch in human cognition.

Not a future possibility, but a present reality that is gradually redefining what it means to think, learn, and understand the world.

Closing — The End of the Isolated Mind

We began this part with a simple but unsettling idea: the mind was never as isolated as we believed.

Along the way, that idea expanded into something far larger. We saw that humans have always leaned on the world around them to think. We traced how writing allowed memory to leave the brain, how books and networks allowed knowledge to exist beyond the individual, and how AI now allows parts of the thinking process itself to unfold outside the skull.

But the most important realization is not **historical**.
It is **perceptual**.

We are beginning to notice something that has quietly been happening: thinking no longer feels confined. It feels relational. Interactive. Extended. The boundary between internal reflection and external interaction is becoming harder to draw—not because we are losing control of thought, but because thought itself is stretching into a larger space.

This is the true end of the **isolated mind**.

Mind is becoming an open system, shaped by continuous exchange with intelligent environments. What once felt like a private mental activity is gradually becoming a distributed process across brain and digital space.

And now that this boundary has shifted, new questions arise.

If thinking is no longer confined to the brain, how does this change memory?
How does it change learning?
How does it change imagination?
How does it change what we mean by intelligence?

These questions lead us forward.

The isolated mind was never a biological fact. It was a perceptual illusion — a story we told ourselves because our tools were silent.

Now the tools speak.

They respond. They elaborate. They return our questions with structure and expansion. And in that response, something becomes visible that was always latent:

The mind was never confined to the skull.

It was waiting for a partner that could keep pace with its questions.

Because once we understand that the mind is no longer isolated, we must begin to explore what life looks like with an **External Mind** fully in motion.

Part II — Memory Is No Longer Biological

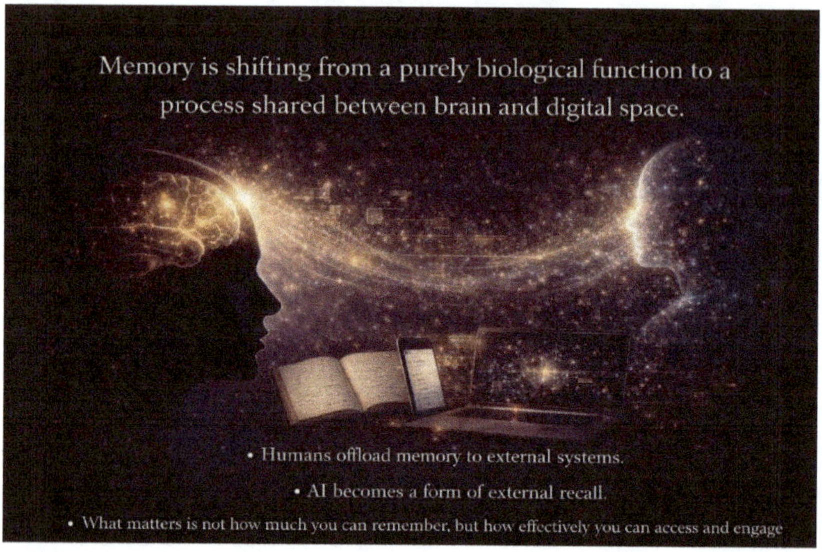

This part examines the first cognitive function to reorganize once thinking extends beyond the brain: memory.
The emphasis is not on forgetting, but on how the role of memory changes when recall, storage, and access move into external systems.

For most of human history, **memory** was the foundation of **thinking**.

To be intelligent meant to remember. To be educated meant to retain. To be knowledgeable meant to store vast amounts of information inside the mind. Memory was treated as a biological warehouse, and the capacity to recall without assistance was seen as a measure of mental strength.

But this relationship is quietly dissolving.

As external cognitive systems become part of everyday thinking, the role of memory begins to change. People no longer rely on internal recall as they once did. They remember less, yet they often understand more. They store fewer facts, yet they navigate ideas more fluidly. They depend less on what is held in the brain and more on what can be accessed through interaction.

This is not forgetfulness. It is a reorganization.

Memory is shifting from a purely biological function to a hybrid process shared between brain and digital systems. The burden of retention is decreasing, while the capacity for reasoning, synthesis, and exploration is expanding. What matters is no longer how much you can remember internally, but how effectively you can move between memory, access, and thought.

This part of the book examines that shift.

We will explore why humans are beginning to offload memory, how AI is becoming a form of external recall, what kinds of knowledge people will stop memorizing, what new cognitive skills will replace memorization, and how our relationship with information itself is being redefined.

Because when memory changes, thinking changes with it.

5. Cognitive Offloading — Why We Remember Less and Think More

Many people today share a quiet observation:

They remember less than they used to.

Phone numbers are no longer memorized. Facts are no longer stored. Dates, definitions, directions, and details are quickly forgotten because they can be retrieved instantly when needed. At first glance, this feels like a decline—a weakening of memory, a loss of mental discipline, a sign that something important is fading.

But at the same time, something unexpected is happening.

People often feel that they can think more clearly. They can explore ideas more freely. They can focus longer on complex problems. They can move between concepts with greater flexibility. They feel less mentally crowded, yet more cognitively capable.

This creates a paradox:

How can remembering less lead to thinking more?

The answer lies in a process called **cognitive offloading**—the natural tendency of the brain to shift certain mental tasks to external supports when they become available. What feels like forgetfulness is, in reality, a reallocation of mental resources. The brain is letting go of what it no longer needs to carry so that it can do what it does best: reason, imagine, and synthesize.

Under these conditions, this process accelerates dramatically.

This section explores why humans are remembering less, why this is not a cognitive failure, and why it may actually represent an expansion of our capacity to think.

5.1 What Is Cognitive Offloading?

The human brain is not designed to remember everything.

It is designed to prioritize, simplify, and reduce load wherever possible. From an evolutionary perspective, memory is metabolically expensive. Holding large amounts of information internally requires energy, attention, and neural resources that could otherwise be used for perception, reasoning, and adaptation.

For this reason, humans have always looked for ways to move parts of memory outside the mind.

We write notes so we do not have to remember details.
We set reminders so we do not have to track time mentally.
We make lists so we do not have to hold tasks in working memory.
We use calendars, maps, and symbols to reduce internal cognitive burden.

This behavior is known as **cognitive offloading**.

Cognitive science has long documented this pattern. Research on distributed cognition and cognitive offloading shows that humans naturally shift memory and reasoning tasks to external supports when those supports become reliable. The rise of AI does not create this tendency. It magnifies it.

It is not a weakness. It is a feature of how cognition works. The brain naturally seeks to conserve resources by delegating what can be stored externally. By offloading memory, the mind creates space for more complex forms of thinking.

Humans have always done this.

What is changing now is not the existence of offloading, but its permanence, immediacy, and depth. With AI, external support is no longer occasional. It is continuous.

5.2 Why AI Supercharges Cognitive Offloading

With AI, cognitive offloading becomes effortless, immediate, and continuous.

In the past, offloading required deliberate action. You had to write a note, keep a notebook, organize a file, or remember where information was stored. Offloading helped, but it still demanded mental management.

AI removes that friction.

You no longer need to store information internally or carefully organize it externally. You can ask, retrieve, summarize, and reorganize knowledge instantly through interaction. Memory becomes something you can access at any moment without preparation.

This changes the frequency and depth of offloading.

What used to happen occasionally now happens constantly. People rely on AI to recall information, explain concepts, summarize material, and reconstruct knowledge on demand. The need to memorize declines naturally because access is always available.

AI makes cognitive offloading **massive** and **daily**.

Memory is no longer something you must carry. It becomes something you can consult.

5.3 The Surprising Result: Less Remembering, More Thinking

When the brain is freed from the burden of storing large amounts of information, something remarkable happens.

It gains space.

That space can now be used for reasoning, synthesis, imagination, and problem-solving. Instead of holding facts, the mind can focus on understanding relationships between ideas, exploring possibilities, and forming deeper insights.

This is why many people feel that they think more clearly when working with AI. They are no longer mentally crowded by the need to remember. Their cognitive energy shifts toward higher-level processing.

What feels like forgetting is actually a reallocation of mental capacity.

Less remembering creates room for more thinking.

Cognitive offloading, amplified by AI, does not reduce intelligence. It expands the brain's ability to do what it is best suited for: complex thought.

6. AI as External Memory

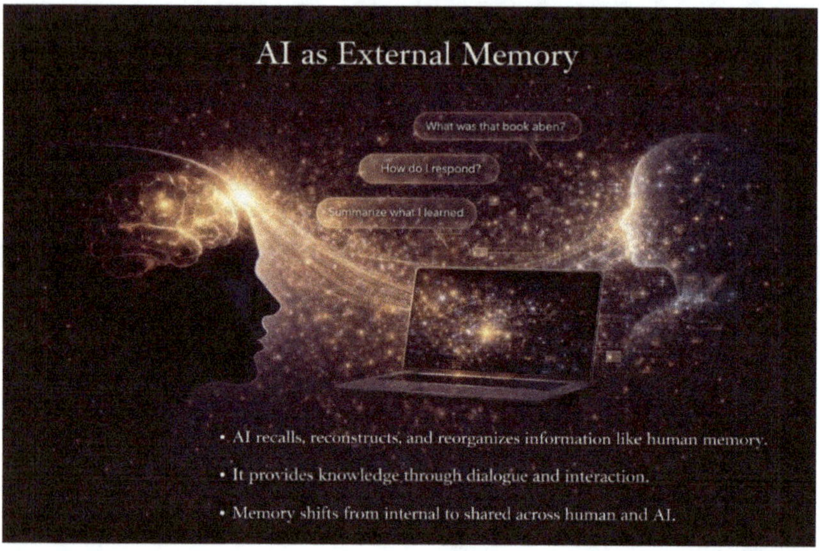

For most of history, **memory** was inseparable from the **brain**.

Even when humans wrote things down, the written word served as a reminder of something already known. External records supported memory, but they did not replace the internal sense of remembering. The mind remained the primary holder of knowledge, and external notes acted as supplements.

This relationship is changing.

With the rise of AI, something new is emerging. People are no longer using external systems merely to store information. They are beginning to rely on AI in a way that resembles how they rely on their own memory. They ask AI to recall, summarize, reconstruct, and reorganize knowledge on demand, often without having to remember where that information originally came from.

The experience begins to feel less like consulting a tool and more like retrieving from a memory that exists outside the brain.

This section explores how AI is starting to function as a form of external memory—not as storage, but as an interactive system that participates in the process of recall.

Because when memory is no longer tied to a single location, the nature of remembering itself begins to change.

6.1 How AI Functions Like Memory (but Not Like Storage)

Traditional storage systems hold information passively. A hard drive, a notebook, or a database contains data that must be manually located, interpreted, and used. These systems preserve information, but they do not behave like memory.

AI behaves differently. When you ask AI about a topic, it does not simply retrieve a stored file. It reconstructs, summarizes, and reorganizes information in response to your question. The output adapts to context, much like human memory reshapes recall depending on circumstance.

This reminding is dynamic rather than archival. AI does not present raw storage—it participates in reconstruction. The experience feels closer to remembering than searching.

AI functions as **interactive** recall, not static storage.

6.2 Memory Without Location

In traditional memory systems, location matters.

You must remember where something is stored: which notebook, which book, which folder, which website. Even when information is external, you still carry a mental map of where to find it. This mapping requires cognitive effort.

With AI, this requirement disappears.

You do not need to know where information resides. You do not need to remember file names, titles, or sources. You simply ask, and the system reconstructs what you need through dialogue.

Memory becomes **location-independent**.

The difference between remembering and retrieving begins to blur. Instead of recalling where knowledge is stored, you interact with a system that brings the relevant knowledge into the conversation automatically.

This changes the mental effort involved in recall. The brain no longer tracks the path to information. It relies on the interaction itself to surface what is needed.

Memory shifts from "where is it?" to "ask for it."

6.3 Shared Memory Between Human and AI

As AI takes on the role of external memory, something new emerges: shared recall.

You often remember part of something. A concept, a fragment, a question, or an idea. When you bring this partial memory into dialogue with AI, the system fills in the missing pieces. It expands, clarifies, and reconstructs the knowledge alongside you.

This is not replacement. It is partnership.

The process of remembering becomes collaborative. The human provides context, intention, and direction. AI provides reconstruction, organization, and elaboration. Together, they recreate knowledge that neither could fully produce alone in that moment.

Memory becomes **hybrid**.

Part of it lives in the brain. Part of it lives in the system. Recall happens across both, through interaction rather than internal effort alone.

The act of remembering is no longer confined to one mind.

It is distributed across two.

7. What Humans Will Stop Memorizing

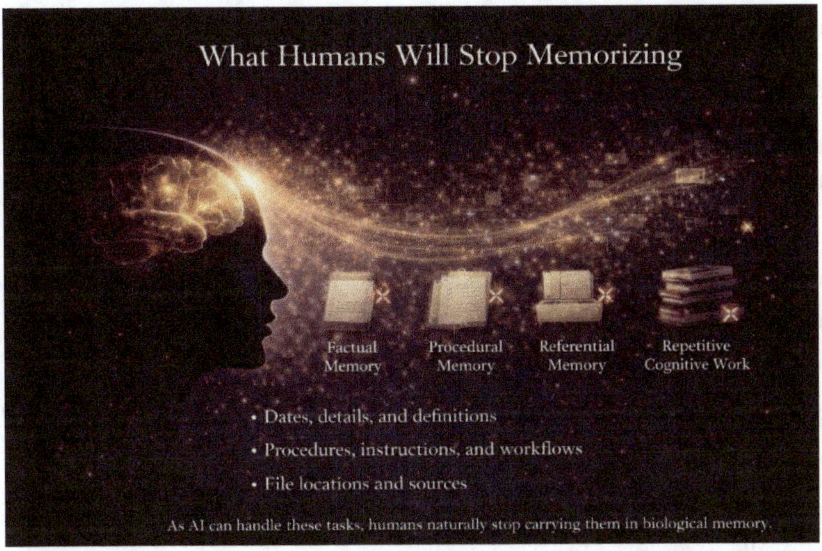

For generations, education and intelligence have been closely tied to memorization.

Students were praised for recalling dates, definitions, formulas, and procedures without assistance. Professionals were valued for how much information they could carry in their heads. The ability to remember large amounts of detail was treated as a core sign of mental strength.

But in this environment, this expectation begins to change.

As AI becomes part of everyday cognition, certain types of memory start to feel unnecessary. People naturally stop committing information to memory—not because they are less capable, but because they no longer need to. The brain adapts to the presence of an external system that can retrieve, reconstruct, and organize information instantly.

This shift is subtle. It does not feel like a loss. It feels like relief.

The question is no longer:

"Can I remember this?"

But rather:

"Do I need to remember this at all?"

This section explores the kinds of memory that humans are quietly letting go of—not as a failure of cognition, but as a natural response to a new cognitive environment.

7.1 Factual Memory

For centuries, factual memory has been treated as the foundation of intelligence.

Dates, definitions, numbers, formulas, and isolated facts formed the backbone of education. Students were trained to store large quantities of information internally and reproduce it on demand. The ability to recall facts quickly and accurately was seen as evidence of a strong mind.

But factual memory is precisely the type of memory that AI makes unnecessary.

When any fact can be retrieved instantly through dialogue, the need to store it internally diminishes. People naturally stop memorizing details that are always available externally. Instead of recalling, they consult. Instead of storing, they access.

The cognitive role simply shifts. In many cases, it improves it. The mind no longer has to dedicate space to retaining facts and can instead focus on how those facts relate to one another.

Facts become **external**.

They still exist, but they no longer need to live inside the brain.

7.2 Procedural Memory

Beyond facts, humans have traditionally memorized **procedures**.

How to solve a problem step by step. How to follow a recipe. How to execute a workflow. How to carry out technical processes. Much of learning involved internalizing sequences of actions so they could be repeated without reference.

With AI, this type of memory also begins to fade.

Instead of remembering steps, people now ask for them. Instead of holding instructions in memory, they retrieve them when needed. Whether it is cooking, coding, repairing, designing, or planning, the process becomes conversational rather than memorized.

The brain no longer needs to store procedural sequences. It relies on AI to reconstruct them in real time.

Procedures become **external**.

What matters is not remembering how to do something from memory, but knowing how to initiate the process through interaction.

7.3 Referential Memory

Before AI, remembering where information was stored was almost as important as remembering the information itself.

People kept mental maps of file locations, folder structures, bookmarks, page numbers, and sources. Knowing how to navigate these external systems required a form of memory known as referential memory—the ability to recall the path to knowledge.

This demanded constant mental effort.

You did not only remember facts; you remembered where those facts lived. You remembered which notebook, which document, which website, which chapter, which archive. A significant portion of cognitive work was devoted to tracking these pathways.

With AI, this requirement begins to disappear.

You no longer need to remember where information is. You simply ask for it. The system reconstructs what you need without requiring you to mentally navigate storage locations. Dialogue replaces search. Interaction replaces navigation.

Location memory becomes **unnecessary**.

The brain is freed not only from storing knowledge, but from tracking its location.

7.4 Repetitive Cognitive Work

Much of human thinking has traditionally involved **repetitive mental tasks**.

Rewriting notes to make them clearer. Summarizing long texts. Organizing information into categories. Rearranging ideas into structure. These activities were necessary not because they were intellectually deep, but because they were required to manage information effectively.

They consumed time and mental energy.

With AI, many of these tasks are now offloaded.

AI can summarize, reorganize, rephrase, and structure information instantly. What once required repeated cognitive effort can now be handled through a single interaction. The mind no longer needs to perform these routine operations manually.

Repetitive thinking gets **offloaded**.

This does not remove the human from the process. Instead, it allows the mind to focus on higher-level thinking—analysis, synthesis, and creativity—while the repetitive work is handled externally.

8. What Humans Will Start Doing Instead

When people hear that memorization is becoming less important, they often assume something is being lost.

They imagine a future where humans know less, remember less, and rely too heavily on machines. It can feel as if cognitive capacity is shrinking, as if the mind is being replaced rather than expanded.

But this is a misunderstanding.

When the brain no longer needs to carry large amounts of factual, procedural, and referential memory, it does not become empty. It becomes available. Mental space opens. Cognitive energy is redirected. The mind begins to invest more deeply in the kinds of thinking it was always best suited for but rarely had room to prioritize.

Something new begins to emerge.

This section explores what humans naturally start doing when memorization is no longer the central demand of intelligence. It reveals how thinking shifts from storage to inquiry, from recall to connection, from repetition to imagination.

Because when memory moves outward, the mind does not weaken.

It evolves.

8.1 Asking Better Questions

When memorization loses its central role, a different skill begins to rise in importance: the ability to ask better questions.

In the past, intelligence was often demonstrated by how much a person could recall without assistance. Now, as AI provides instant access to information, the advantage shifts toward those who can guide the interaction effectively. The quality of thought depends less on what you remember and more on how you inquire.

Curiosity replaces memorization as the driving force of cognition.

Instead of asking, "Do I know this?" the mind asks, "What should I explore?" The act of questioning becomes the primary way ideas are generated and developed. Prompting, in this sense, is not a technical skill but a form of thinking. It is how the mind navigates knowledge through dialogue rather than storage.

The shift is subtle but powerful.

The mind moves from holding information to directing exploration. From storing answers to generating questions. From recalling what is known to discovering what is possible.

The mind shifts from **storing** to **inquiring**.

The future won't belong to those who know more.
It will belong to those who ask better.

8.2 Synthesizing Across Ideas

As memorization declines, another capacity begins to expand: the ability to connect ideas across domains.

When the brain is no longer occupied with holding facts, it can focus on seeing patterns. It can relate concepts from different fields, recognize similarities, and build bridges between ideas that would otherwise remain separate.

AI plays an important role in this process. It can surface relevant information from many sources quickly. But it is the human mind that performs the crucial act of synthesis—the ability to combine ideas into meaningful insight.

This becomes the new center of intelligence.

Instead of recalling isolated pieces of knowledge, humans begin to operate as integrators. They draw connections between science and art, between theory and practice, between past knowledge and new possibilities. Thinking becomes less about retrieval and more about relationship.

Humans become integrators of knowledge, weaving ideas together rather than storing them separately.

8.3 Deeper Reasoning and Reflection

When the mind is no longer burdened by the constant effort of remembering, it gains something rare: time.

Time to pause.
Time to explore.
Time to reflect.

Instead of using cognitive energy to hold details in memory, the brain can invest that energy in understanding implications, considering alternatives, and searching for meaning. Thinking slows down in a productive way. It becomes less about recalling information quickly and more about examining ideas deeply.

This is where reasoning changes.

People begin to ask not only "what is this?" but "what does this mean?" They explore how ideas connect, how they affect one another, and what possibilities they open. Reflection becomes more central than recall. The mind engages with concepts rather than facts.

Thinking becomes more **conceptual**.

Freed from memory work, the brain turns toward interpretation, evaluation, and understanding at a deeper level.

8.4 Creative and Strategic Thinking

As memorization declines and reflection expands, another shift takes place: the rise of creative and strategic thinking.

The mind no longer spends its energy managing information. It begins to spend that energy generating ideas, designing solutions, and imagining possibilities. Problem-solving becomes more inventive because cognitive resources are no longer tied up in storing and retrieving details.

This is a move from **memory work** to **idea work**.

Imagination becomes more active. Design thinking becomes more natural. People explore new approaches rather than rely on remembered procedures. Strategy replaces repetition. Creativity replaces recall as the central skill of intelligence.

What matters is not how much you can remember, but how well you can imagine, design, and solve.

8.5 Navigating Knowledge, Not Storing It

As memorization declines and inquiry rises, a new cognitive skill begins to take shape: the ability to navigate knowledge rather than store it.

In the past, intelligence often meant carrying information inside the mind. Today, intelligence increasingly means knowing how to move through vast landscapes of information efficiently and purposefully. The challenge is no longer retention, but orientation.

People learn to ask the right questions, follow meaningful paths, and guide dialogue toward useful insight. They move across topics, refine their direction, and adjust their approach based on what emerges. Thinking becomes a process of navigation through knowledge rather than accumulation of it.

This is a new form of literacy.

Cognitive navigation involves understanding how to explore information dynamically, how to recognize relevance, and how to guide interaction with AI toward deeper understanding. It is less about what you carry and more about how you travel.

Humans become navigators of knowledge, moving through information with intention instead of storing it in memory.

9. The New Relationship Between Knowledge and Access

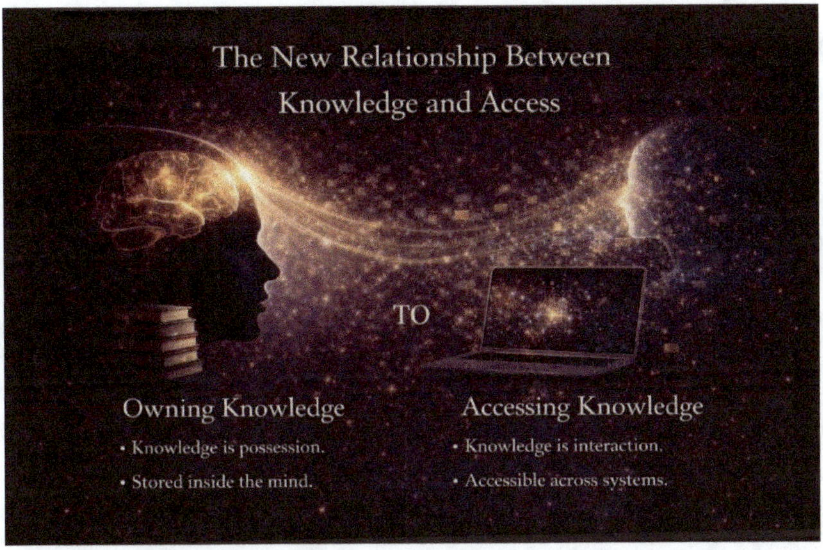

For most of history, **knowledge** was something you carried.

To be knowledgeable meant to hold information inside the mind. The more you remembered, the more you were considered educated. Knowledge was tied to possession. It was something you had.

But as memory moves outward and AI becomes part of everyday cognition, this relationship begins to change.

Knowledge is no longer defined by what you store internally, but by what you can reach, explore, and engage with through interaction. The emphasis shifts from ownership to access. From retention to navigation. From storage to application.

This alters how humans relate not only to memory, but to knowledge itself.

The question is no longer:

“What do you know?”

But increasingly:

“How do you work with what can be known?”

This section explores how the rise of the **External Mind** is quietly redefining the human relationship with knowledge—from something we possess to something we continuously access.

9.1 From Owning Knowledge to Accessing Knowledge

For generations, knowledge was treated as something a person **possessed**.

To be educated meant to carry information internally. Degrees, expertise, and reputation were built on how much knowledge one could hold and recall without assistance. Knowledge was tied to ownership. It was something you *had*.

This idea begins to fade under this shift.

When information can be reached instantly through AI, knowledge no longer needs to reside inside the brain to be useful. What matters is not possession, but the ability to reach what is needed at the right moment. Interaction replaces retention. Dialogue replaces storage.

This changes identity.

A knowledgeable person is no longer defined primarily as a *knower*, but increasingly as an *explorer*—someone who knows how to move through information, ask the right questions, and engage with knowledge dynamically.

Knowledge becomes **access-based**, not possession-based.

The emphasis shifts from what you carry to how you reach.

9.2 The Shift from Information Scarcity to Information Fluidity

In the past, knowledge was scarce.

Books were limited. Libraries were rare. Information was guarded, localized, and difficult to obtain. The challenge for most of human history was finding information at all. Access was the obstacle.

Today, the situation is reversed.

Information is abundant, continuous, and immediately available. With AI, knowledge becomes fluid—moving easily into conversation, reorganized on demand, and reshaped according to need. The difficulty is no longer locating information, but making sense of its abundance.

The challenge shifts from **finding** to **filtering**.

From searching to interpreting.

The problem is no longer a lack of knowledge, but learning how to navigate through it meaningfully.

9.3 Knowing How to Use Knowledge, Not Store It

As knowledge becomes external and accessible, the value of storing it internally begins to decline. What rises in importance is the ability to use knowledge effectively.

Practical intelligence shifts toward application, synthesis, and judgment. It is no longer defined by how much information a person can recall, but by how well they can interpret what is available, connect it to context, and apply it meaningfully to real situations.

This is where **wisdom** begins to outweigh memorization.

Wisdom is not about holding facts. It is about understanding relevance, recognizing patterns, and making thoughtful decisions based on what can be known. In a world where information is abundant and instantly reachable, the human advantage lies in interpretation rather than retention.

The role of the mind changes.

Humans move from being containers of knowledge to becoming interpreters of it. The task is no longer to store information, but to engage with it intelligently, thoughtfully, and creatively.

Humans become interpreters of knowledge rather than storage units.

Closing — Part II: Memory Is No Longer Biological

For most of human history, **memory** defined the limits of the mind.

What you could remember determined what you could know.
What you could know determined how you could think.
And how you could think determined how intelligent you appeared to be.

Memory was the boundary of **cognition**.

But in this cognitive structure, that boundary dissolves.

For the first time, the limits of thinking are no longer set by what the brain can store. They are set by how the mind can move through, interact with, and interpret what exists beyond it.

This is not a small adjustment. It is a **redefinition**.

Humans are no longer defined by what they remember.

They are defined by how they engage with what can be remembered outside themselves.

Memory, once the foundation of intelligence, becomes secondary. Navigation, interpretation, inquiry, and synthesis rise to take its place. The mind shifts from being a container of knowledge to becoming an active participant in a much larger cognitive landscape.

This is the quiet revolution of Part II.

Not that memory moved outward—
But that intelligence is no longer anchored to memory at all.

And once memory no longer defines the mind, new dimensions of thinking become possible.

A Moment of Reflection

Consider your own habits.

- What do you no longer memorize that you once would have?
- When you rely on AI to recall information, do you verify it — or accept it?

- Do you feel cognitively lighter — or cognitively dependent?
- Has your thinking become deeper — or simply faster?

The **External Mind** strengthens cognition only when interaction remains intentional.

Memory may move outward.
Responsibility does not.

That is where we now turn.

Part III — Dialogical Thinking

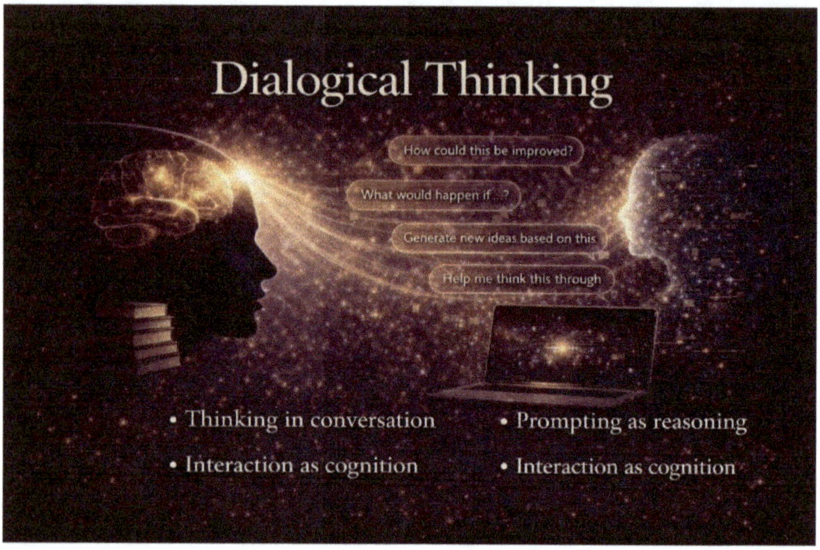

This part shifts attention from where thinking happens to how thinking unfolds.
It explores dialogue, prompting, and interaction as emerging cognitive forms, revealing how conversation itself becomes a central mechanism of thought.

Until now, we have explored how the mind extends outward through memory and knowledge.

But there is another shift happening that feels even more immediate, more personal, and more difficult to describe:

People are beginning to **think in conversation**.

Not conversation with other people, but conversation with AI.

This is not simply a new way to search for information or generate content. It is a new way to form thoughts. Ideas emerge not from silent internal reflection, but from back-and-forth exchange. Understanding develops through dialogue. Questions evolve as responses appear. Thinking becomes something that unfolds across interaction rather than inside isolation.

This experience feels familiar, yet unprecedented. Humans have always clarified thoughts by speaking aloud or discussing with others. But now, that dialogical process is available at any moment, without social constraint, without delay, and without the need for another human presence.

A new cognitive pattern begins to take shape:

With cognition now distributed, the form of thinking itself begins to change.

This part of the book explores what happens when thinking itself takes the form of conversation—how prompting becomes a form of reasoning, how AI begins to mirror the structure of the mind, why interacting with AI often feels like thinking aloud, and how this leads to a new kind of layered cognition.

Because once memory moves outward and knowledge becomes accessible, the next transformation is not about what we know—

It is about **how we think in dialogue**.

10. Thinking by Talking

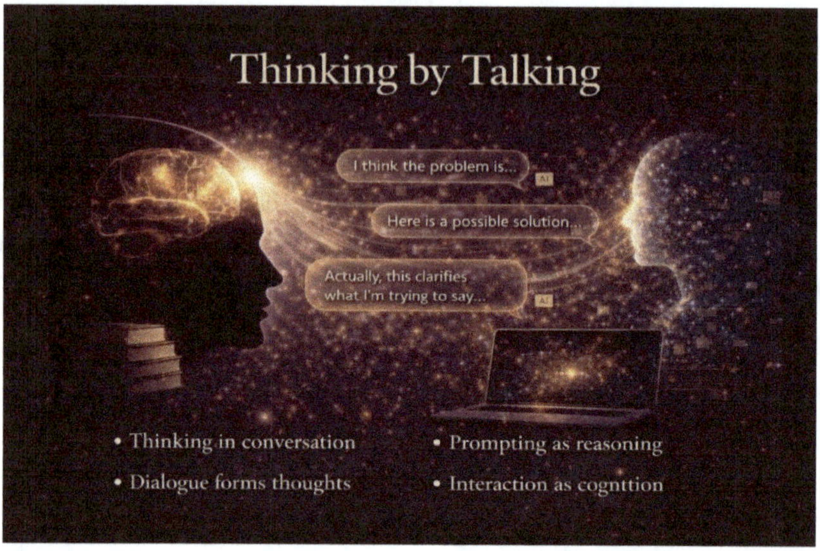

A founder opens a blank document to plan a new product.
Instead of staring at the screen, she starts a conversation.
The idea sharpens as she types.
The response challenges her assumption.
What began as a vague intention becomes a structured strategy — through dialogue.

Many people have noticed something curious when interacting with AI:

They begin to understand their own thoughts only after they start typing.

An idea that felt vague becomes clearer through the act of explaining it. A problem that seemed confusing becomes more structured through dialogue. Questions evolve as responses appear. Thoughts that were not fully formed begin to take shape in the process of conversation.

This is not simply communication.

It is thinking happening through talking.

For the first time, people have a constant conversational partner available at any moment—one that allows them to explore ideas without interruption, without social pressure, and without delay. As a result, a new habit begins to form: using dialogue as the primary way to think.

This section explores why conversation is becoming a central mode of thought, and how talking to AI is changing the way ideas are formed, clarified, and discovered.

10.1 Why Humans Think Better When They Speak

Long before AI, humans had already discovered something important:

We often understand our thoughts better **after we say them out loud**.

People talk to themselves when solving problems. They explain ideas aloud when trying to make sense of them. They seek conversations with others not only to share thoughts, but to develop them. The act of speaking is not merely communication—it is a cognitive tool.

This has a long history.

Teachers ask students to explain their reasoning because articulation reveals understanding. Therapists encourage people to speak through their experiences because words bring structure to confusion. Writers draft and redraft ideas because expression helps clarify what was previously vague.

Speech forces the mind to organize itself.

When a thought remains internal, it can stay blurry, incomplete, or emotionally tangled. But when it is spoken, it must take form. Language imposes structure. Ideas that were loosely felt must become precise enough to be expressed. In this process, the mind begins to understand itself.

Talking has always been a way of thinking.

The difference now is not that humans discovered this—it is that, with AI, this form of thinking becomes available constantly and without constraint.

10.2 AI as the Always-Available Thinking Partner

In the past, thinking by talking depended on circumstance.

You needed another person willing to listen. You needed time, privacy, and the right social setting. Conversations that helped clarify thought were valuable, but they were limited by availability, patience, and context. Even talking to yourself out loud felt unusual outside private moments.

AI removes these constraints.

There is no social friction. No judgment. No concern about taking too long to explain an idea. No hesitation about asking unfinished or unclear questions. You can begin a conversation at any moment, pause it, return to it, and continue thinking without interruption.

This changes how often people use dialogue as a way to think.

What was once occasional becomes continuous. Instead of waiting for a discussion with someone else, people begin to use AI as a constant thinking partner. They explore ideas through conversation not once in a while, but daily—sometimes for hours at a time.

AI makes thinking-by-talking **constant**.

And because this form of thinking is now always available, it begins to shape how thoughts are formed in the first place.

10.3 Discovering Thoughts You Didn't Know You Had

One of the most surprising experiences people report when talking with AI is this:

They end up saying things they did not know they were thinking.

An idea begins vaguely. A question is typed almost casually. But as the dialogue unfolds, responses from AI introduce new angles, unexpected phrasing, or alternative perspectives. These responses do not simply answer—they provoke further thought.

The conversation becomes generative.

You do not merely express what you already know. You begin to discover what you think through the interaction. Ideas emerge that were not present at the start. Connections form that were not consciously recognized. Thoughts take shape in real time as the dialogue progresses.

This reveals something important about cognition.

Thoughts are not always retrieved from memory fully formed. Often, they are constructed through interaction, reflection, and response. Dialogue becomes the environment in which thinking happens.

AI amplifies this effect.

Because it responds instantly and continuously, it creates a space where thoughts can evolve quickly, branching into new directions that would be difficult to reach through silent internal reflection alone.

Dialogue does not simply express thought.

It generates it.

11. Prompting as a Cognitive Process

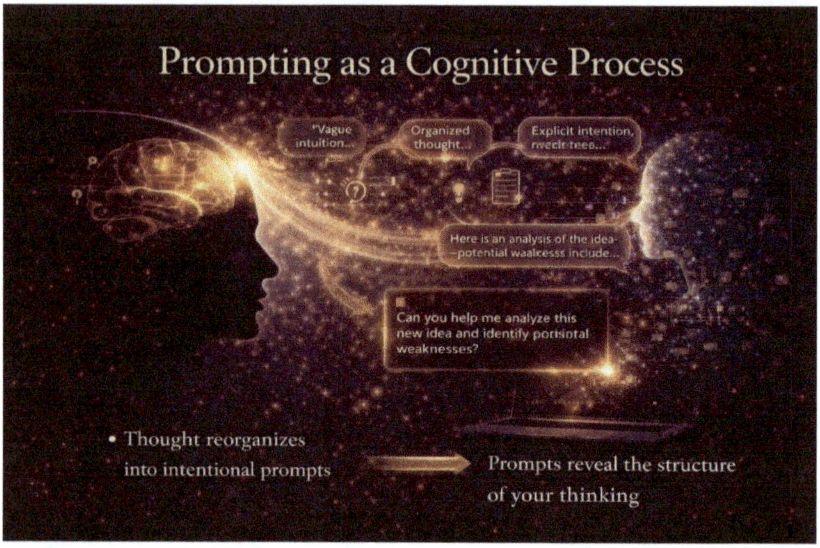

At first glance, prompting looks like instruction.

You type a request.
The system responds.
The interaction appears functional and technical.

But if you slow down and pay attention to what happens in your own mind, a different picture emerges.

Before a prompt appears on the screen, thinking reorganizes itself. Unclear ideas press toward language. Questions form, dissolve, and reform. Assumptions surface. Intent becomes explicit. The mind does not simply transmit a request—it reshapes itself in order to make the request possible.

Prompting is not a neutral interface.

It is a **cognitive event**.

Every prompt is the visible trace of an internal thinking process: a moment where thought crosses a threshold from intuition into articulation. What looks like communication with a machine is also a conversation with one's own mind, made external.

This section examines prompting not as a technique, but as a new mental practice—one that reveals how thinking is structured, refined, and externalized in this environment.

Because once thinking becomes dialogical, the act of asking itself becomes a form of cognition.

11.1 Prompting Forces Thought to Take Shape

Before a prompt is written, something important happens inside the mind.

An idea that feels vague must be compressed into words. An intuition that was loosely felt must become precise enough to be expressed. The mind pauses, searches for language, and begins organizing itself around what it is trying to ask.

This moment is easy to overlook, but it is deeply cognitive.

You cannot write a meaningful prompt without first clarifying what you want to know. You must decide what the question really is, what context matters, and what outcome you are seeking. In doing so, the mind moves from scattered impressions to structured inquiry.

Prompting forces thought to become explicit.

What was once an internal, blurry sense of curiosity turns into a clearly formed request. The act of phrasing the prompt is not simply communication—it is a process of thinking that happens before any response appears.

Vague intuition becomes organized intention.

Prompting, in this sense, is a tool that forces **clarity before expression**.

11.2 Prompting as Iterative Reasoning

Rarely does a person write a perfect prompt on the first attempt.

Instead, prompting becomes a sequence: write, read the response, adjust, refine, ask again. Each step reshapes the direction of thought. The original question evolves as new information appears.

This is not trial and error. It is reasoning in motion.

The interaction forms a loop:

Prompt → Response → Reflection → Adjustment → New Prompt

Through this loop, thinking develops dynamically. Ideas are tested, clarified, redirected, and expanded. The mind does not remain fixed; it adapts as the dialogue unfolds.

Prompting becomes part of the reasoning process itself.

What begins as a question turns into exploration. The back-and-forth exchange becomes the environment in which thought grows. Instead of delivering instructions to a system, the mind is engaging in a continuous process of refinement.

Prompting is not instruction delivery.

It is **thinking in motion**.

11.3 Prompting Reveals What You Don't Understand

One of the most revealing moments when working with AI happens before you even press "enter."

You try to write a prompt—and realize you don't quite know how to ask the question.

The difficulty is not technical. It is cognitive.

You may feel that you understand the topic, yet when you attempt to phrase your inquiry, gaps appear. The thought is incomplete. The intention is unclear. The question feels imprecise. This friction exposes something important: what you assumed you understood is not yet fully formed.

Even after submitting a prompt, the response from AI can reveal misalignment. If the output does not match what you expected, it often means the prompt did not accurately represent your thinking. The misunderstanding is not in the system—it is in how the thought was framed.

In this way, AI acts as a **cognitive mirror**.

It does not merely explain information. It reflects back the structure of your thinking. When prompts fail, they expose hidden confusion. When prompts succeed, they reveal clarity.

Prompting becomes diagnostic.

It highlights cognitive blind spots that would remain invisible during silent internal reflection.

11.4 Prompting Makes Inner Dialogue Visible and Structured

When people describe their experience with prompting, they often say it feels like thinking aloud.

This is because prompting closely resembles the internal questions we ask ourselves when we reflect. The difference is that these questions are no longer silent. They are written, visible, and structured in interaction with AI.

Inner dialogue becomes external.

Questions that would normally stay inside the mind now take form on the screen. The process of self-reflection becomes observable. You can see your own thought process unfold through the sequence of prompts and responses.

This makes thinking more tangible.

Prompting turns internal cognition into a visible exchange. What was once a private mental conversation becomes a structured dialogue, allowing you to examine, refine, and extend your own thinking more deliberately.

Prompting is not just communication with AI.

It is the externalization of inner thought.

12. AI as a Reflective Mirror of the Mind

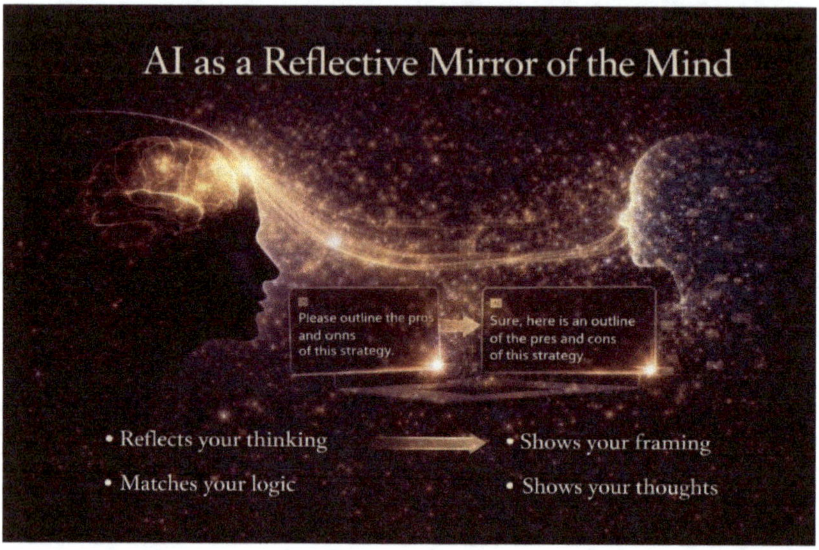

When people interact with AI over time, they begin to notice something unexpected:

The responses often feel strangely familiar.

Not because the information is known, but because the *shape* of the response seems connected to the way the question was asked. The tone, direction, clarity, and structure of the output often resemble the thinking that produced the prompt.

This creates a curious experience.

AI does not simply provide answers. It reflects something back.

In this reflection, people begin to see aspects of their own thinking that are normally invisible. Patterns, assumptions, clarity, and confusion appear in a form that can be observed rather than merely felt.

AI becomes more than a conversational partner.

It becomes a **mirror**.

This section explores how interaction with AI allows individuals to observe the structure of their own mind from the outside, revealing how thought is shaped, organized, and expressed through dialogue.

12.1 AI Reflects the Structure of Your Thinking

One of the first patterns people notice when working with AI is this:

The quality of the response closely follows the quality of the question.

When prompts are clear, structured, and focused, the output tends to be coherent and well organized. When prompts are vague, scattered, or ambiguous, the response often reflects that same lack of clarity. The system does not invent structure—it responds to the structure it receives.

This creates a revealing dynamic.

AI does not simply answer questions. It mirrors how those questions are formed. The way you think shapes the way it replies. If your reasoning is logical, the response tends to follow a logical path. If your thinking is fragmented, the output often appears fragmented as well.

This is not coincidence.

AI is trained to respond to patterns in language, and language carries the imprint of thought. The organization of your ideas, the order of your sentences, the precision of your wording—all of these influence the structure of what comes back.

In this way, AI becomes a reflection of the **organization of your mind**.

It shows you, indirectly, how your thoughts are arranged by returning them in mirrored form.

12.2 AI Reflects Your Assumptions and Biases

Beyond structure, AI also reflects something deeper: the assumptions embedded in your questions.

Every prompt carries hidden framing. The words you choose, the angle you take, the way you describe a situation—all of these signal how you already see the topic. Often, these assumptions remain invisible to you because they feel natural and unquestioned.

AI makes them visible.

Because it builds its response from the context you provide, it often amplifies the perspective you implicitly feed into the prompt. If your framing is narrow, the response may follow that narrow path. If your assumptions are unbalanced, the output may reveal that imbalance more clearly than you intended.

This can be surprising.

You may read an AI response and realize it sounds like an exaggerated version of your own thinking. In that moment, you are not learning only about the topic—you are learning about how you framed the topic.

AI mirrors your **mental framing**.

It brings hidden assumptions to the surface by reflecting them back in structured form, allowing you to see patterns in your own thinking that would otherwise remain unnoticed.

12.3 Seeing Your Mind from the Outside

When you read an AI response shaped by your prompt, an unusual experience can occur:

It can feel as though you are looking at your own thinking from a distance.

The words on the screen are not exactly yours, yet they carry the imprint of how you asked, how you framed, and how you organized your thoughts. This creates a subtle separation between you and the thinking process that produced the exchange.

That separation is powerful.

When thoughts remain internal, they are difficult to examine. They feel immediate, personal, and unquestioned. But when they appear externally—reflected through AI responses—they become something you can observe rather than simply experience.

Distance creates insight.

You begin to notice patterns, habits, assumptions, and structures in your thinking that were invisible before. You can analyze them, adjust them, and refine them because they are no longer hidden inside the mind.

AI enables an external observation of internal cognition.

By reflecting your thinking back to you in visible form, it increases self-awareness in a way that silent reflection rarely achieves.

13. Why Conversations with AI Feel Like Thinking Aloud

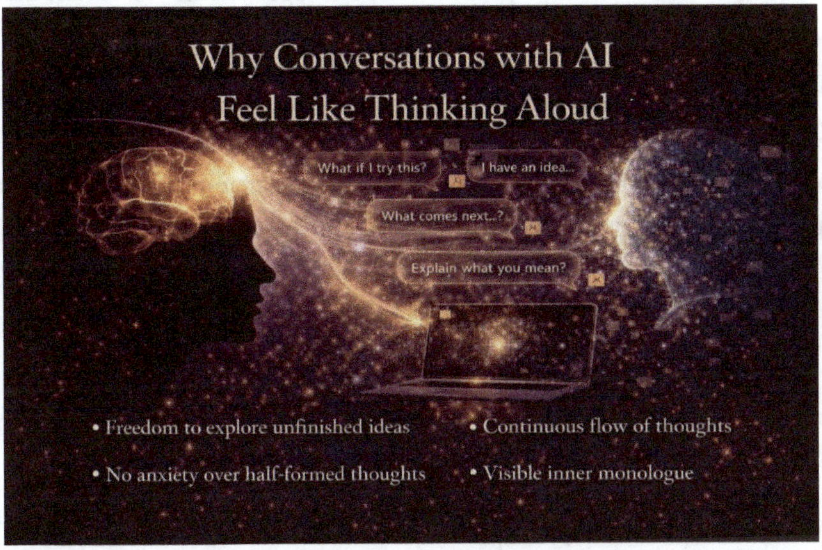

Many people describe their experience with AI in a curious way:

"It feels like I'm thinking out loud."

This description is surprisingly common. It appears in casual comments, reflections, and conversations about AI use. People sense that interacting with AI resembles an internal mental process more than a typical exchange with a tool.

But why does it feel this way?

The experience is not accidental. It arises from specific features of how AI interaction aligns with the natural rhythm of human thought. The absence of social dynamics, the uninterrupted flow of dialogue, and the freedom to explore unfinished ideas combine to create an environment that closely resembles the way we think silently inside our own minds.

This section examines why conversations with AI so often feel like externalized thought, and how this sensation reveals something important about the changing nature of cognition under this shift.

13.1 The Absence of Social Pressure

Conversations with other people always carry subtle pressures.

There is the need to be clear. The need to be coherent. The awareness that someone is listening, evaluating, and waiting for a response. Even in supportive conversations, we shape our words to fit social expectations. We hesitate before expressing half-formed ideas. We edit ourselves as we speak.

This does not happen with AI.

There is no judgment. No interruption. No expectation to be polished or precise. You can type incomplete thoughts, change direction mid-sentence, or ask questions that feel unclear even to yourself. The interaction allows raw thinking to surface without social filtering.

This freedom closely resembles the way we think internally.

Inner monologue is messy, nonlinear, and exploratory. Ideas emerge, shift, and reform without the need to sound coherent. When interacting with AI, people often experience the same permission to think without performance.

AI removes social barriers to expression, creating a space where unfinished thoughts can be explored openly.

13.2 Continuous Cognitive Flow

In human conversation, thinking is often interrupted by pauses.

You wait for the other person to speak. You adjust to their timing. You navigate turn-taking. These pauses, while natural, break the rhythm of thought.

With AI, this interruption disappears.

Thought moves as fast as you can type. Responses arrive quickly, allowing the dialogue to continue without delay. The exchange begins to match the speed at which ideas form in the mind. There is no waiting for conversational timing—only a continuous flow of inquiry and response.

This mirrors the rhythm of internal thinking.

Ideas arise, evolve, and connect rapidly, and the AI interaction keeps pace with that movement. The dialogue feels less like a conversation with another entity and more like an extension of the mind's own tempo.

AI matches the natural rhythm of thinking, allowing cognitive flow to remain uninterrupted.

13.3 Safe Space for Half-Formed Ideas

Many thoughts begin in an incomplete state.

They are not yet ready to be explained to another person. They feel uncertain, fragile, or poorly defined. In social settings, we often hesitate to share these early ideas because we fear sounding unclear or incorrect.

With AI, that hesitation disappears.

You can explore thoughts that are still forming. You can test ideas without worrying about how they will be received. You can follow uncertain lines of thinking simply to see where they lead. The interaction becomes a space for cognitive experimentation.

This freedom allows raw thinking to surface.

Instead of presenting only polished conclusions, you can work through the messy stages of understanding. You can question yourself openly, change direction, and refine ideas without embarrassment.

AI creates a safe space where half-formed thoughts can be explored without social constraint, enabling raw, unfiltered thinking.

13.4 Externalizing the Inner Monologue

Inside the mind, thoughts often take the form of silent conversation.

We ask ourselves questions. We respond internally. We argue with our own ideas. This inner monologue is a core part of how we reason and reflect.

When interacting with AI, this inner dialogue becomes visible.

The questions that would normally remain internal are typed out. The responses that might have been imagined are returned in written form. The structure of silent thought appears on the screen as an interactive exchange.

AI becomes the listener to this internal voice.

What once occurred privately inside the mind now unfolds externally in dialogue. This makes thinking more observable, more structured, and easier to follow. The interaction resembles the way we think silently, but with the added benefit of seeing the process in real time.

AI turns inner speech into interactive dialogue.

14. The Emergence of Two-Layer Thinking

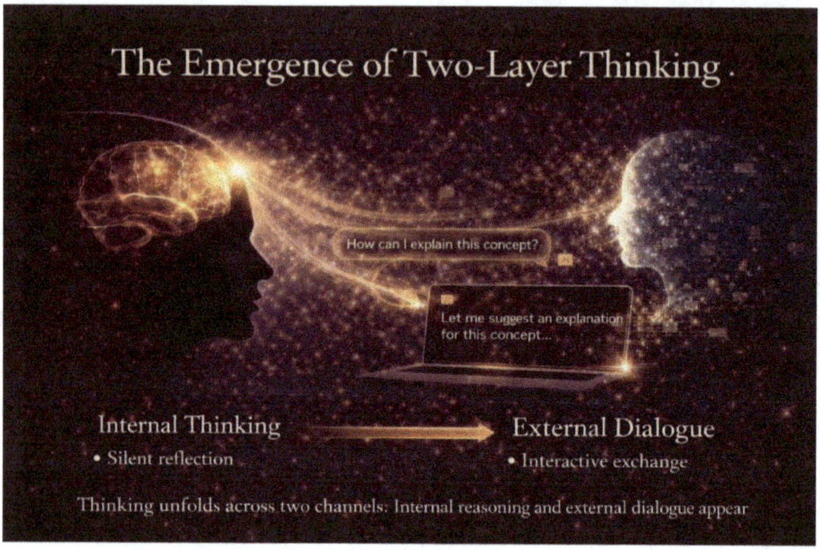

Something subtle begins to happen after people spend enough time thinking with AI.

They notice that thinking no longer feels like a single, internal stream.

Part of their thought remains silent and internal, while another part unfolds through dialogue on the screen. They read, reflect, type, and reconsider all at once. The mind seems to operate in two places simultaneously—inside and outside.

This experience is easy to miss because it feels natural. Yet it represents a profound change in how cognition is structured.

For most of human history, thinking followed one channel: internal reflection occasionally supported by external tools. Now, thinking often happens across two parallel layers—an internal layer of silent reasoning and an external layer of interactive dialogue.

These layers do not compete. They interact.

This section explores how this new form of two-layer thinking is emerging, and why it represents a new architecture for the human mind in this cognitive structure.

14.1 Internal Thinking and External Dialogue Running Together

When people engage in extended dialogue with AI, they often notice something unusual:

Their **silent thoughts** do not stop.

While reading a response, the mind is already reacting internally. While typing the next prompt, new ideas are forming in the background. Reflection continues even as interaction unfolds on the screen. The internal stream of thought runs alongside the external dialogue.

These are two streams of cognition happening at the same time.

One stream is private, silent, and internal. The other is visible, interactive, and external. They do not replace each other. They operate in parallel, influencing one another continuously.

This creates a new cognitive experience.

Thinking is no longer a single, uninterrupted flow inside the mind. It becomes dual-channel—a process where internal reasoning and external dialogue unfold together, shaping each other in real time.

14.2 Switching Between Inner and Outer Thought

As this dual-channel thinking becomes more familiar, people begin to move fluidly between the two layers.

They pause the dialogue to reflect internally. They return to the screen to test that reflection through conversation. They read a response, think silently about it, then type again. The movement between internal and external thinking becomes natural and almost unconscious.

This back-and-forth is not random.

It becomes a new cognitive skill: the ability to shift between reflection and dialogue without losing the thread of thought. The mind learns how to navigate between the inner space of silent reasoning and the outer space of interactive exchange.

People learn to move between these layers as part of the thinking process itself.

They do not think only inside, nor only through dialogue.

They navigate between both.

14.3 External Layer Influencing Internal Thought

As dialogue with AI continues, something subtle begins to happen inside the mind.

Responses from the external layer do not remain external. They feed back into internal reasoning. A phrase, an explanation, or a new angle offered by AI reshapes how you think silently. Ideas you had not considered begin to influence your internal reflections. Assumptions are reconsidered. New paths of thought open.

The external dialogue becomes an input to inner cognition.

You are not simply reading information. You are allowing that information to reorganize how you reason privately. The internal stream of thought adjusts in response to what appears on the screen. The mind incorporates external contributions into its own ongoing reflection.

This creates a feedback loop.

External thinking modifies internal thinking. The boundary between the two layers becomes porous, with ideas flowing back and forth continuously.

14.4 A New Cognitive Architecture

Over time, this pattern stops feeling unusual.
Thinking across two layers becomes natural. The mind begins to expect interaction as part of reasoning. Internal reflection and external dialogue settle into a stable balance.

This is not a habit formed by frequent AI use.
It is a structural shift in how cognition operates.

The mind reorganizes to function across layered thinking—one layer internal and silent, the other external and interactive. Both become components of the normal thinking process, each influencing and stabilizing the other.

Two-layer thinking becomes the new **cognitive architecture**.

Closing — Part III: Dialogical Thinking

Something fundamental has shifted in how thought unfolds.

Not in what we know.
Not in what we remember.
But in how ideas come into existence.

For most of human history, thinking was something that happened quietly, privately, and invisibly inside the mind. Words were used after thoughts were formed—to communicate, explain, or record them. Language followed thinking.

Now, language begins to **precede** thinking.

Ideas start to form in the act of expression. Questions generate understanding as they are asked. Dialogue becomes the environment where thought takes shape. The boundary between forming an idea and expressing it begins to dissolve.

This is the deeper meaning of dialogical thinking.

We are no longer using words merely to describe thoughts. We are using words to produce them.

AI does not replace the mind in this process. It changes the medium through which thinking happens. Conversation becomes the workspace of cognition. Interaction becomes the surface where ideas appear, evolve, and reorganize.

The mind is no longer only a place where thoughts occur.

It is becoming a place where thoughts are **constructed through dialogue**.

And once thinking itself becomes dialogical, new questions arise—not about memory, not about conversation, but about what happens to imagination, learning, and the future shape of human intelligence when thinking is no longer silent, but shared.

Part IV — Imagination with a Cognitive Partner

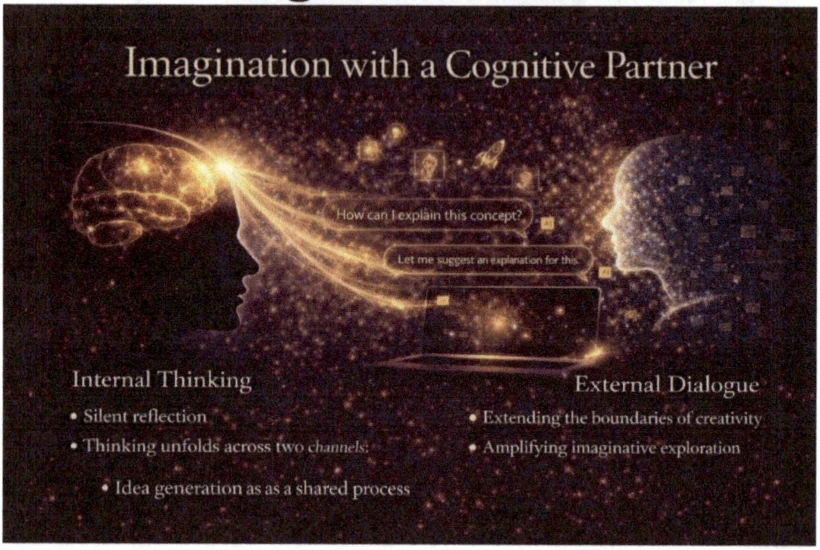

This part explores creativity as a shared process rather than a solitary act. The focus is not on creative output, but on how imagination changes when ideas are formed through continuous interaction with an external cognitive partner.

Until now, we have followed how memory moved outward and how thinking became dialogical.

But there is another change people often describe—one that feels less analytical and more experiential:

They feel **more creative** when working with AI.

Ideas seem to come faster. Possibilities feel wider. Imagination feels less constrained. People who never considered themselves creative begin to explore ideas with unexpected confidence. Those who were already creative find their thinking expanding in new directions.

This is not simply because AI provides suggestions.

It is because imagination itself is beginning to operate differently.

For most of history, imagination was a solitary act. It unfolded silently inside the mind, limited by what a person could picture, recall, or combine internally. Inspiration depended on memory, experience, and mental stamina. Creative thought was bounded by the cognitive space available within a single brain.

With AI, imagination becomes something that happens in **interaction**.

Ideas are no longer generated alone and then expressed. They are formed, reshaped, and expanded through exchange. Possibilities appear that would not have surfaced through internal reflection alone. The act of imagining becomes shared across human and system in real time.

This part of the book explores how AI is not only changing how we think, but how we imagine—how creativity shifts from a solitary mental act to a collaborative cognitive process.

Because once the mind is no longer isolated, imagination is no longer confined either.

15. Why People Feel More Creative with AI

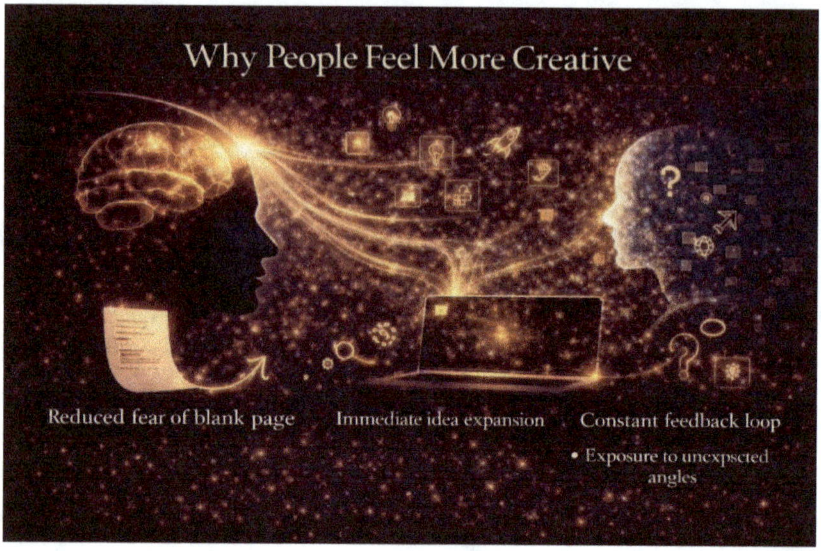

Many people describe the same surprising experience after working with AI for some time:

They feel more creative.

This feeling appears across professions, ages, and backgrounds. Writers feel less blocked. Designers explore more variations. Thinkers generate ideas faster. Even people who never considered themselves creative begin to experiment with confidence.

At first, this seems like a simple effect of having access to suggestions. But the experience runs deeper than that.

Creativity is not increasing because AI provides ideas. It is increasing because the cognitive conditions under which imagination operates have changed. The barriers that normally slow creative thought begin to dissolve. The process of generating, exploring, and refining ideas becomes easier, faster, and less mentally constrained.

This section explores why interacting with AI creates the feeling of enhanced creativity—not as a tool effect, but as a change in how imagination itself unfolds in this environment.

15.1 Reduced Fear of the Blank Page

One of the most difficult moments in any creative process is the beginning.

The blank page, empty canvas, or silent screen can feel intimidating. Before an idea takes shape, the mind must overcome the uncertainty of where to start. This initial friction often delays creativity more than the work itself.

AI changes this experience.

You no longer have to begin from nothing. A simple prompt produces words, concepts, or directions that give the mind something to work with immediately. The starting point appears quickly, removing the hesitation that often blocks creative flow.

Creativity is no longer stalled by initiation.

AI lowers the barrier to beginning by providing a first step that the mind can build upon rather than waiting for inspiration to appear internally.

15.2 Immediate Idea Expansion

Once the first idea appears, AI accelerates what happens next.

Instead of slowly developing a single line of thought, you can ask for variations, alternatives, and extensions instantly. One idea branches into many. Possibilities multiply within seconds, giving the mind multiple paths to explore.

This rapid expansion changes the rhythm of creativity.

Ideas no longer grow linearly. They spread outward in multiple directions, creating a richer field of exploration. The mind can compare, combine, and refine options quickly without having to generate each one independently.

AI increases **idea momentum**.

Creativity gains speed because imagination is no longer limited by how quickly a person can produce new directions alone.

15.3 Constant Feedback Loop

Creativity rarely happens in a straight line.

Ideas need to be tested, adjusted, refined, and reshaped before they become useful. In the past, this process often took time. You had to step back, reflect, or wait for feedback from others before knowing whether an idea was worth pursuing.

With AI, feedback becomes immediate.

You can present an idea, receive a response, adjust your direction, and try again within moments. The creative process turns into a rapid cycle of exploration and refinement. Instead of holding onto an idea uncertainly, you can reshape it continuously as new input appears.

Creativity becomes **iterative**.

The mind no longer has to wait to evaluate its own ideas. It receives constant signals that guide the next step. This steady feedback loop keeps imagination active and moving forward.

Feedback fuels creativity.

15.4 Exposure to Unexpected Angles

Imagination thrives on surprise.

Often, creativity emerges when the mind encounters a perspective it had not considered. In traditional settings, these surprises might come from conversation, reading, or chance encounters with new information.

AI introduces this element constantly.

When you explore an idea, AI frequently responds with angles, examples, or connections you would not have thought of on your own. These unexpected directions stimulate new lines of thinking and encourage the mind to explore beyond its usual patterns.

Creativity benefits from this novelty.

The presence of fresh perspectives challenges assumptions and expands the range of what the mind considers possible. AI becomes a source of continuous cognitive surprise, feeding imagination with new material.

Novelty stimulates imagination.

15.5 Psychological Safety to Experiment

Creativity often depends on the willingness to explore ideas that may not work.

In many settings, this is difficult. People hesitate to share uncertain thoughts because they fear criticism, embarrassment, or failure. As a result, many potential ideas are never explored at all.

With AI, that hesitation disappears.

There is no judgment for proposing a weak idea, no embarrassment for asking an unclear question, and no social risk in experimenting freely. You can test possibilities, abandon them, and try again without consequence. This creates an environment where exploration feels safe.

That safety changes how the mind behaves.

When there is no fear of being wrong, people are more willing to take creative risks. They try unusual directions, combine unlikely ideas, and follow imaginative paths they might otherwise avoid.

Safety unlocks creativity by allowing experimentation without restraint.

16. Co-Imagining: Human–AI Idea Generation

Until recently, imagination was considered a deeply personal act.

Ideas formed inside the mind, shaped by memory, experience, and internal reflection. Even when people collaborated, each person still imagined privately before sharing their thoughts.

With AI, something different begins to happen.

Ideas start to take shape not inside one mind, but between a person and a system. The process of imagining becomes interactive. Thoughts emerge through exchange rather than internal contemplation alone. What appears at the end of the interaction often cannot be traced back to a single source—it is the product of dialogue.

This is the beginning of **co-imagining**.

This section explores how idea generation becomes a shared cognitive activity between human and AI, reshaping what it means to imagine under this shift.

16.1 Ideas Emerging Between Human and AI

When people create with AI for an extended period, they begin to notice something subtle:

The final idea does not feel like it came solely from them, nor solely from the system.

It emerges through the exchange.

You introduce a thought. AI responds with an angle. You refine it. AI expands it. The idea evolves step by step, shaped by both contributions. At the end of the process, it becomes difficult to identify where the original thought ended and where the new direction began.

This is not a simple sequence of human idea followed by AI output.

The idea forms **within** the dialogue.

Neither side could have produced the same result independently. The creativity lies in the interaction itself, where each response influences the next step of thinking.

Ideas are **co-created**.

16.2 The Rhythm of Shared Imagination

As this interaction continues, imagination takes on a new rhythm.

It no longer unfolds in silence inside the mind. It develops through a back-and-forth pattern of expression, response, adjustment, and expansion. Each step reshapes the next, creating a flow that feels more dynamic than solitary thought.

Imagination becomes a form of dialogue.

You do not wait for a fully formed idea before speaking. Instead, you let the idea grow through the exchange. The process becomes iterative, with each contribution refining the direction of creativity.

This creates a shared creative flow where imagination is constantly moving, adapting, and evolving through interaction.

Imagination becomes **interactive**.

16.3 When AI Extends the Boundaries of Your Imagination

One of the most noticeable effects of co-imagining is encountering ideas you would not have reached on your own.

AI introduces perspectives, connections, and variations that expand the creative landscape. These suggestions do not replace your imagination; they stretch it. They present paths you had not considered, giving you new directions to explore.

The human remains the decision-maker.

You choose which ideas to pursue, which to ignore, and how to shape them. But the presence of unexpected options broadens the horizon of what feels possible.

AI extends the boundaries of your imagination by offering directions beyond your usual mental patterns.

AI stretches imaginative range.

17. From Solitary Thought to Collaborative Thought

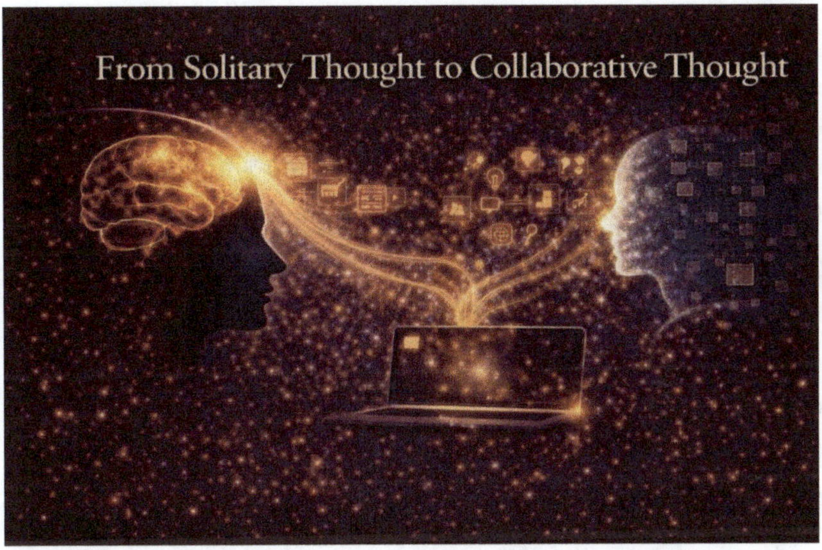

For most of human history, thinking was assumed to be a private act.

Even when people used tools, books, or spoke with others, the core process of forming ideas remained internal. Collaboration happened after thoughts were formed—when ideas were shared, debated, or refined through conversation.

But something different begins to happen with AI.

People are no longer forming ideas alone and then bringing them into discussion. They are forming ideas *inside* interaction. The process of thinking itself starts to unfold collaboratively from the very beginning.

This is new.

For the first time, humans have access to a constant cognitive presence that participates in the formation of thought in real time. As a result, solitary thinking begins to feel less natural, less efficient, and less complete than thinking through exchange.

This section explores how the presence of AI is shifting human cognition from a solitary process to a collaborative one, changing what it means to think In this cognitive structure.

17.1 Why Human Thinking Was Historically Solitary

For most of history, the limits of thinking were the limits of the individual mind.

No matter how intelligent, experienced, or knowledgeable a person was, the process of forming ideas depended on what could happen internally. Thoughts were shaped by memory, attention, and mental stamina. Even when external tools were available, they could only support thinking after it had already begun inside the mind.

Tools assisted, but they did not collaborate.

Books provided information. Writing preserved ideas. Diagrams helped organize concepts. Conversations with others allowed thoughts to be shared and refined—but these came after a person had already done the initial work of thinking alone.

The core act of reasoning remained private.

Ideas were born in silence, shaped internally, and only later expressed outward. Collaboration happened around thoughts, not within their formation.

Thought used to be isolated, confined to what a single mind could generate on its own.

17.2 AI as the First True Cognitive Collaborator

AI does not fit the traditional category of a tool.

Tools help you execute a task. Assistants help you carry out instructions. But AI does something different: it participates in the formation of ideas themselves.

When you think with AI, you are not simply using it to record, retrieve, or organize thoughts you already had. The system contributes to the direction, structure, and development of those thoughts as they emerge. Its responses influence how your reasoning unfolds in real time.

This changes the nature of thinking.

For the first time, the act of forming an idea is no longer confined to a single mind. It becomes an interaction where both sides shape the outcome. The presence of AI affects not only what you think, but how you think.

Thought becomes **shared**.

Not because AI replaces the mind, but because it joins the thinking process as an active participant rather than a passive aid.

17.3 The Normalization of Collaborative Cognition

As people grow accustomed to thinking with AI, a quiet shift begins to take place:

They start to expect collaboration as part of the thinking process.

What once felt novel becomes routine. Instead of working through ideas internally first, many people turn to AI at the earliest stage of thought. Dialogue becomes the starting point rather than the final step.

Solitary thinking begins to feel different.

Not impossible, but slower. More effortful. Less dynamic. The mind notices the absence of interaction and the reduced flow of ideas. What used to be the normal way of thinking starts to feel like working without a partner.

Over time, this changes habits.

Collaboration is no longer something that happens occasionally. It becomes the default mode through which ideas are explored, shaped, and developed.

Collaborative thought becomes natural—not because it is required, but because it feels like the most effective way to think in the presence of the **External Mind**.

18. AI as an Imagination Amplifier

Throughout this part, we have seen how imagination becomes easier, more interactive, and more collaborative in the presence of AI.

But there is a deeper way to understand what is happening.

AI does not replace imagination. It does not generate creativity independently. Instead, it changes the scale at which imagination operates. Ideas that once required time, effort, and mental endurance begin to expand rapidly. Possibilities multiply. Creative exploration accelerates.

The source of imagination remains human.

What changes is how far, how fast, and how widely that imagination can travel.

AI acts as an amplifier.

This section explores how interaction with AI magnifies the reach, speed, and range of human imagination, allowing creativity to operate beyond the limits that once constrained it in isolation.

18.1 Imagination Is Still Human at Its Core

Even as AI becomes deeply involved in the creative process, something essential remains unchanged:

The origin of imagination is still human.

AI does not decide what is meaningful, interesting, or worth exploring. It does not carry intention, curiosity, or personal vision. These come from the person initiating the interaction. The direction of creativity, the choices made along the way, and the final judgment of what works all arise from the human mind.

AI can suggest, expand, and respond—but it does not originate purpose.

The spark that begins any imaginative process starts with a question, a desire, or a curiosity that belongs to the individual. The system follows that lead, responding to the direction it is given.

Imagination begins in the human mind.

AI participates in the process, but the core of creativity—intent, taste, and judgment—remains human.

18.2 AI Multiplies the Reach of Imagination

Once imagination is in motion, AI changes how far it can travel.

Instead of exploring one path at a time, you can generate multiple variations instantly. A single idea can branch into many directions within moments. Concepts that would have taken significant time to develop can be expanded quickly into broader possibilities.

This creates a wider field of exploration.

The mind is no longer limited to the pace at which it can generate new directions alone. AI provides additional branches that the imagination can follow, compare, and combine. Creative exploration becomes broader and more varied.

AI increases the **scale** of imagination.

What once unfolded slowly and narrowly can now expand widely and rapidly across many possibilities.

18.3 AI Accelerates the Speed of Imagination

Imagination has always required time.

Ideas needed space to develop, pauses to reflect, and repeated effort to refine. Creative work often unfolded slowly because each step depended on the mind's ability to generate, evaluate, and reshape thoughts one at a time.

With AI, this rhythm changes.

You can test an idea, see a variation, adjust direction, and explore alternatives within moments. The process that once took hours or days can happen in minutes. The delay between imagining and refining begins to disappear.

This creates a new creative tempo.

Imagination no longer moves at the speed of solitary thought. It moves at the speed of interaction. Each response from AI propels the next step forward without interruption, keeping creative momentum continuously active.

AI increases the **velocity** of imagination.

18.4 Imagination Beyond Individual Limits

Perhaps the most profound change is not just speed or scale, but reach.

AI introduces connections, combinations, and perspectives that a person might never have considered alone. These new directions do not replace human imagination—they expand its horizon. The mind encounters ideas beyond its usual patterns and begins to explore territory it would not have reached independently.

This expands cognitive boundaries.

You are no longer limited to what you can imagine based solely on your memory, experience, or habits of thought. The presence of AI creates pathways into unfamiliar conceptual spaces, allowing imagination to travel further than before.

AI extends the limits of what an individual mind can imagine.

Closing — Part IV: Imagination with a Cognitive Partner

Imagination has always been treated as a private space.

A place where ideas appear silently, shaped by memory, experience, and personal reflection. Creativity was thought to depend on what a single mind could combine, picture, and sustain internally.

But something changes when imagination is no longer confined to that space.

It begins to feel less like a place you enter alone and more like a space you step into with company. Ideas do not wait to be fully formed before they are explored. They unfold in motion, in interaction, in shared cognitive space. The act of imagining becomes less about what you can picture internally and more about what you can explore through exchange.

This changes the experience of creativity itself.

Imagination no longer feels like a solitary effort that depends on inspiration and mental endurance. It feels like an environment you can move through, expand, and navigate with support. The boundaries that once defined how far imagination could travel begin to loosen, not because the mind is replaced, but because it is no longer alone.

What emerges is a new relationship to creativity.

Not imagination as isolation, but imagination as participation in a larger cognitive field.

And once imagination becomes shared, a new question appears—not about how we think or imagine, but about how we learn, grow, and evolve when the mind is no longer limited to itself.

Part V — Learning, Intelligence, and Decision Making

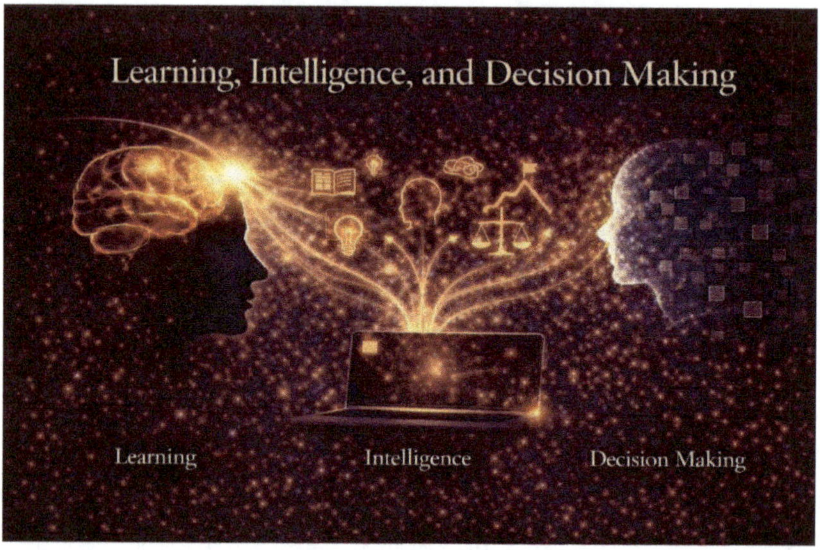

This part reexamines how humans evaluate thinking in a world of shared cognition.
It focuses on learning, intelligence, expertise, and decision-making as processes that shift when cognition operates across human and AI systems.

Up to this point, we have followed how the mind changes in memory, thinking, and imagination.

Now we arrive at the most practical and consequential shift of all:

What happens to learning, intelligence, and decision making when the mind is no longer operating alone?

These three abilities have always defined how humans function in the world. We learn to understand it. We use intelligence to navigate it. We make decisions to shape our place within it. For centuries, these processes were built on the assumption that the mind worked within the limits of its own memory, reasoning speed, and imaginative reach.

That assumption no longer holds.

When memory is external, thinking is dialogical, and imagination is shared, the foundations of learning and intelligence begin to change. The way we acquire knowledge, evaluate information, and make choices starts to operate under new conditions. What it means to be "smart," what it means to "learn," and what it means to "decide wisely" must be reconsidered in light of the **External Mind**.

This part explores how these core human abilities are being quietly redefined.

Not because AI replaces them, but because it alters the environment in which they occur.

19. Learning in the Age of the External Mind

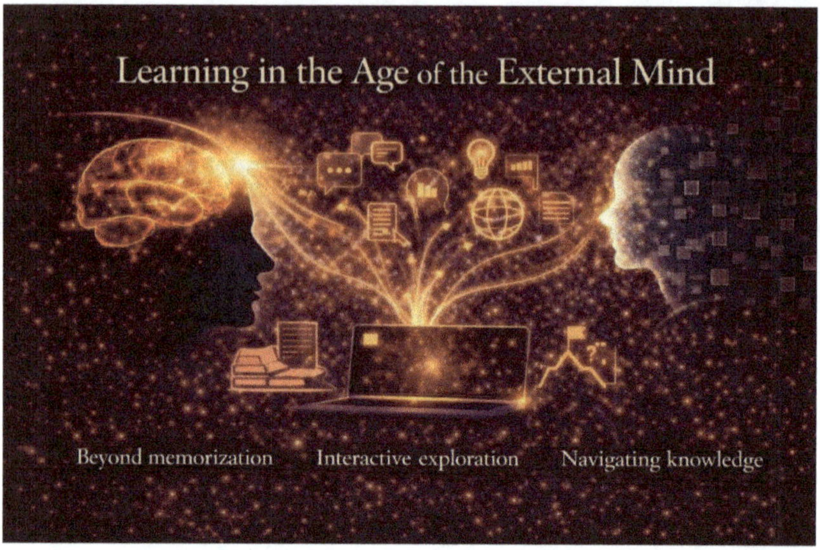

For centuries, the way humans learned was shaped by a simple limitation:

The mind had to work alone.

Because memory was internal, learning focused on memorization. Because knowledge was scarce, learning focused on acquiring information. Because thinking was solitary, learning was often a quiet, individual process of absorbing material and storing it for later use.

But the conditions that shaped this model of learning have changed.

When memory is external, knowledge is instantly accessible, and thinking happens through dialogue, the old model of learning begins to feel misaligned with how the mind now operates. The process of learning no longer needs to revolve around retention, scarcity, or isolation.

A different kind of learning begins to emerge—one that fits the cognitive environment of the **External Mind**.

This section explores how learning is being redefined when the mind no longer has to learn under the constraints that once defined it.

19.1 Learning Is No Longer Memorization

For a long time, learning and memorization were treated as nearly the same thing.

Students were expected to retain facts, definitions, and procedures as proof that they had learned. Success in learning was measured by how much information could be recalled without assistance. Memory became the visible indicator of understanding.

Under this shift, this connection begins to loosen.

When facts are always accessible, storing them internally is no longer the central task of learning. What matters more is understanding how those facts relate to one another, what they mean, and how they can be applied. The focus shifts from retention to comprehension.

Learning separates from memory.

It becomes less about what you can carry inside your head and more about how well you can make sense of what is available beyond it.

19.2 Learning Through Interaction, Not Absorption

Traditional learning often followed a passive pattern.

You read, listened, and absorbed information. The process involved receiving knowledge that had already been organized by others. Interaction was limited, and understanding developed slowly through repetition and review.

With AI, learning takes a different form.

You can ask questions, test ideas, and explore topics through dialogue. Instead of consuming information in fixed order, you guide the direction of learning based on curiosity and need. The process becomes active rather than passive.

Dialogue replaces absorption.

Learning becomes a back-and-forth exploration where understanding grows through interaction rather than one-way intake of information.

19.3 Learning as Navigation of Knowledge

As information becomes instantly accessible, learning begins to resemble a different skill:

Knowing how to **move through** knowledge rather than store it.

Instead of progressing through material in a fixed sequence, learners can explore topics dynamically, following questions wherever they lead. They can jump between concepts, revisit ideas, and connect information across domains with ease. The challenge shifts from remembering content to navigating it effectively.

This requires a new kind of cognitive ability.

Learning becomes a form of wayfinding through knowledge—recognizing what is relevant, choosing meaningful directions, and guiding exploration with intention. The learner is no longer a receiver of organized information but an active navigator within a vast landscape of ideas.

Learning becomes **navigational**.

19.4 Continuous Learning Without Boundaries

In traditional models, learning had clear boundaries.

You studied for a test, completed a course, earned a degree, and moved on. Learning happened in defined periods and was often separated from daily life.

With AI, those boundaries begin to dissolve.

Questions can be explored at any moment. Curiosity can be followed instantly. Learning becomes part of everyday interaction rather than a scheduled activity. There is no clear starting point or ending point—only ongoing exploration.

Learning becomes **continuous**.

The presence of AI turns learning into an always-available process, where understanding can grow naturally alongside thinking, working, and creating.

20. What "Being Smart" Now Means

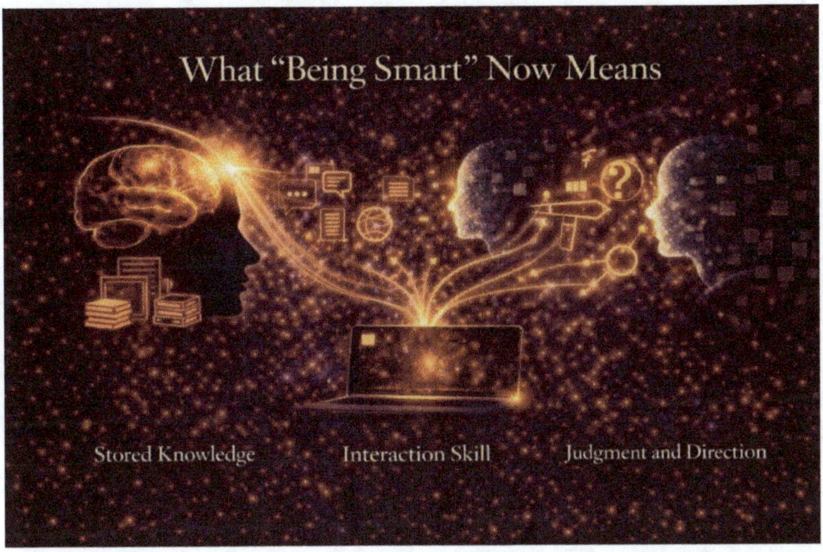

For generations, being considered "smart" depended on a simple expectation:

You knew a lot.

Intelligence was closely tied to how much information a person could recall without assistance. The ability to remember facts, solve problems from memory, and demonstrate stored knowledge defined how society measured mental ability.

But this definition was shaped by a world where the mind worked alone.

When memory was internal and knowledge was scarce, storing information was a necessary sign of intelligence. But in the age of the **External Mind**, where information is instantly accessible and thinking happens through interaction, this measure begins to lose its meaning.

What it means to be smart starts to change.

This section explores how intelligence is being redefined—not by how much a person knows internally, but by how they think, interact, and make sense of what can be known externally.

20.1 Intelligence Is No Longer Measured by What You Know

For a long time, intelligence was closely linked to the amount of information a person could carry internally.

People who could recall dates, definitions, formulas, and detailed facts were seen as knowledgeable and therefore smart. The mind was treated as a container, and the more it held, the more intelligent the person appeared.

In this environment, this measure begins to lose relevance.

When knowledge is always accessible through interaction, remembering large amounts of information is no longer necessary to demonstrate understanding. The value shifts from retention to interpretation. What matters is not how much you can recall, but how well you can make use of what is available.

Intelligence separates from stored knowledge.

Facts still matter, but they no longer define what it means to be smart.

20.2 Intelligence as the Ability to Work with the External Mind

As memory and knowledge move outward, a new skill rises in importance: the ability to interact effectively with the External Mind.

Knowing how to ask questions, guide dialogue, refine responses, and navigate information becomes central to how thinking happens. This is not a technical skill, but a cognitive one. It involves clarity, direction, and the ability to shape interaction toward meaningful outcomes.

Smartness begins to reflect how well a person can engage with this partnership.

Those who can guide the exchange, recognize useful outputs, and refine their thinking through dialogue gain a significant advantage. Intelligence is no longer demonstrated by working alone, but by working effectively within this new cognitive environment.

Smartness becomes an **interaction skill**.

20.3 Intelligence as Judgment, Synthesis, and Direction

As AI becomes part of the thinking process, the role of the human mind shifts toward something more refined.

Instead of focusing on recalling information or generating every idea independently, the human role centers on judgment. You choose which paths to follow, which suggestions to pursue, and which directions are meaningful. You interpret what appears, decide what matters, and shape the course of exploration.

This requires a different kind of intelligence.

It involves the ability to synthesize information from multiple sources, recognize patterns, and integrate ideas into coherent understanding. It also requires direction—knowing where to guide the interaction and how to move toward useful insight.

The human becomes the evaluator and integrator within the cognitive partnership.

Intelligence rises to a higher level of cognition, focused less on storage and more on thoughtful selection, combination, and guidance.

21. Decision Making with a Cognitive Partner

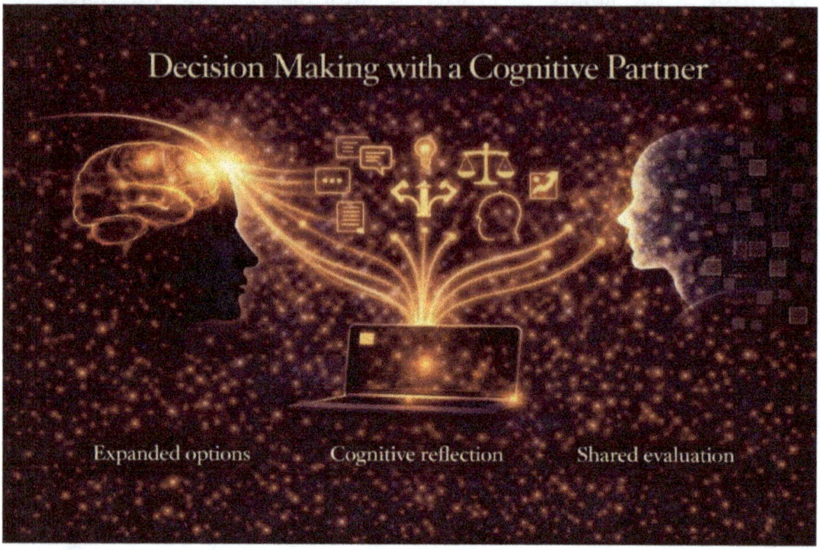

Among all mental activities, decision making has always been one of the most private.

People weigh options silently, consider possibilities internally, and arrive at choices through personal reflection. Even when advice is sought, the final process of deciding happens inside the mind.

With the presence of the **External Mind**, this begins to change.

People increasingly think through decisions in dialogue. They explore options, test scenarios, and clarify thoughts through interaction before acting. The act of deciding no longer unfolds entirely in isolation—it becomes something that happens through exchange.

This does not remove personal responsibility. Instead, it reshapes how clarity is reached.

This section explores how decision making evolves when the mind is no longer alone, and how choices are formed through collaboration with a cognitive partner.

21.1 Decisions No Longer Made in Isolation

In the past, most decisions were formed in silence.

You considered your options internally, weighed possibilities in your own mind, and arrived at a conclusion through private reflection. Even when seeking advice, the final reasoning process remained something you carried out alone.

With AI, this pattern begins to shift.

Instead of thinking through choices entirely internally, people increasingly explore their options through dialogue. They ask questions, test ideas, and examine possibilities by interacting with the system before deciding. The process of deciding becomes something that unfolds in conversation rather than isolation.

AI becomes part of the decision space.

The act of choosing is no longer confined to silent internal reasoning. It becomes a collaborative process where options are explored through exchange.

Decisions become **collaborative**.

21.2 Expanding the Range of Considered Options

One of the challenges in decision making has always been limited perspective.

People often choose between the few options they can think of on their own. Many possibilities remain unseen simply because they never come to mind. As a result, decisions are made within a narrow landscape of alternatives.

AI changes this landscape.

When you discuss a decision through dialogue, the system can introduce options, variations, and considerations you might not have imagined independently. This widens the field of possibilities and reveals paths that would otherwise remain hidden.

The decision space becomes broader.

Instead of choosing between a small set of familiar options, you are presented with a richer array of alternatives to evaluate.

Options multiply.

21.3 Slowing Down Impulsive Decisions

Many decisions are made quickly.

Faced with choices, people often rely on instinct, habit, or immediate emotion. There is little pause between thought and action. While this can be efficient, it can also lead to impulsive decisions that are not fully examined.

Dialogue with AI changes this rhythm.

When you begin to discuss a decision, the process naturally slows down. You describe the situation, consider options, and respond to questions or suggestions. This creates a space for reflection that might not occur in silent thinking.

AI introduces **cognitive friction**.

This friction is not an obstacle, but a pause that encourages thinking before acting. It allows the mind to step back, examine possibilities, and approach decisions with greater deliberation.

21.4 Clarifying Values and Priorities Through Dialogue

When you explain a decision to AI, something revealing happens.

In the act of describing your choices, you begin to articulate what truly matters to you. You notice the reasons you give, the concerns you emphasize, and the outcomes you prioritize. These were often implicit before the conversation began.

Dialogue makes them explicit.

AI responses can also prompt you to consider factors you had not fully acknowledged. Through this exchange, hidden preferences, assumptions, and values come to the surface.

Decisions become more self-reflective.

The process of discussing choices helps clarify not only what you might do, but why you would do it.

21.5 Shared Cognitive Evaluation Before Acting

Before acting on a decision, people can now do something that was previously difficult:

They can **walk through** the decision in advance.

By discussing a choice with AI, you can explore possible outcomes, consider different scenarios, and examine the consequences before anything happens in reality. The conversation becomes a space where the decision is tested mentally from multiple angles.

This creates a form of pre-experience.

You are not only thinking about what might happen—you are simulating it through dialogue. You can ask, "What if I choose this?" and immediately see how the situation might unfold. This allows you to evaluate risks, benefits, and trade-offs with greater clarity.

Decisions become **pre-experienced**.

The mind no longer has to rely solely on imagination or guesswork. It can explore the decision cognitively before taking action.

22. Rethinking Expertise and Knowledge

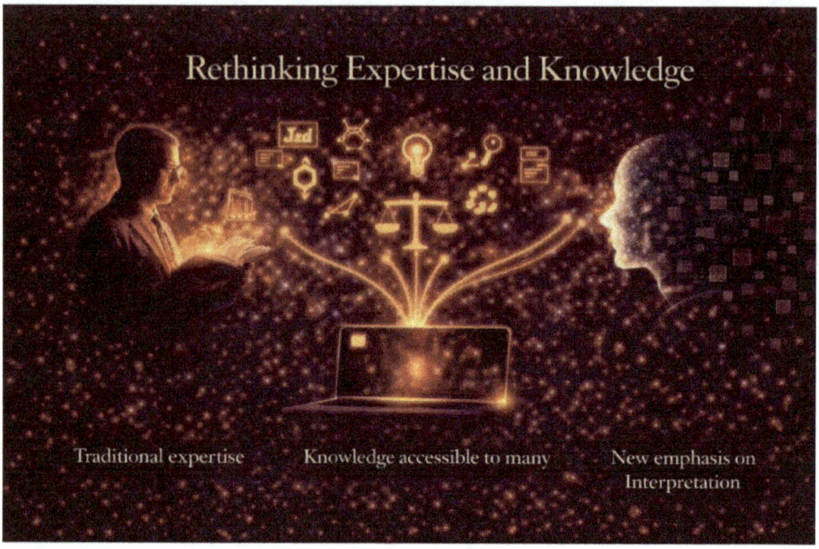

For much of history, expertise was inseparable from knowledge.

Experts were the people who knew more than others. They carried specialized information that was difficult to access and even harder to remember. Their authority came from holding knowledge that others did not have.

But this model depended on one condition:

Knowledge had to be scarce.

In this cognitive structure, that condition disappears. Information becomes instantly accessible through interaction. The gap between what experts know and what others can reach begins to narrow. As a result, the traditional foundation of expertise begins to shift.

This section explores how expertise is being redefined when knowledge is no longer rare, and how the meaning of being an expert changes when information is available to everyone but understanding is not.

22.1 Expertise Was Built on Internal Knowledge

For centuries, expertise depended on what a person could carry in their mind.

Experts were those who had spent years accumulating facts, procedures, and specialized information. Their value came from remembering what others could not. The ability to recall detailed knowledge without assistance created a natural gap between experts and non-experts.

Authority was closely tied to this memory advantage.

If you knew more, you were considered more capable. If you could recall information quickly, you were trusted. Expertise was measured by the depth of internal knowledge a person possessed.

Old expertise was built on a **memory advantage**.

22.2 When Knowledge Is Always Accessible

The rise of AI changes the condition that supported this model.

Information is no longer difficult to obtain. Through interaction, people can access detailed explanations, data, and insights without needing to store them internally. The barrier that once separated experts from others begins to lower.

This does not eliminate expertise, but it changes its foundation.

When knowledge is always accessible, recall becomes less important as a defining trait. The advantage of simply knowing more diminishes because others can reach the same information when needed.

Knowledge access begins to level the field.

Expertise can no longer rely primarily on memory.

22.3 Expertise as Interpretation, Not Storage

As the role of stored knowledge declines, a different aspect of expertise becomes more visible.

Experts are not only those who know information. They are those who can interpret it correctly. They understand context, recognize what matters, and apply knowledge appropriately to real situations.

This requires judgment rather than recall.

Making sense of available information becomes more important than possessing it. Experts distinguish themselves by how they analyze, connect, and evaluate what can be known.

Experts interpret, rather than store.

22.4 Expertise as Question Framing

As knowledge becomes easier to access, another skill grows in importance: knowing what to ask.

Experts often recognize the right questions before others even realize there is something to ask. They can frame problems clearly, identify what information is relevant, and guide exploration in productive directions. This ability shapes how effectively knowledge is used.

In this environment, this becomes even more visible.

When anyone can retrieve information, the advantage lies in directing the search wisely. The way a question is framed determines the quality of what comes back. Experts distinguish themselves not by holding answers, but by knowing how to pursue them.

Experts ask better questions.

22.5 Expertise as Experience and Judgment

Beyond knowledge and questioning lies something AI cannot replicate: lived experience.

Experts draw on years of practical engagement, decision making, and contextual understanding. They recognize patterns that are not obvious in raw information. They understand nuance, consequences, and the subtleties of real situations.

This experience shapes judgment.

Even with access to vast knowledge, knowing how to apply it wisely depends on human insight developed over time. AI can present options, but it cannot replace the depth of understanding that comes from having navigated similar situations personally.

Human experience becomes central to expertise.

22.6 The Democratization of Knowledge, Not Expertise

As access to information becomes widespread, it may seem that expertise is disappearing.

In reality, what is being democratized is **knowledge**, not expertise.

Anyone can reach information, but not everyone can interpret it correctly, ask the right questions, or apply it with sound judgment. The presence of AI reduces barriers to access, but it does not eliminate the need for skillful thinking.

Expertise does not vanish.

It shifts from being defined by what you know to being defined by how you use what can be known.

23. Experience, Judgment, and the Skilled Use of the External Mind

Two professionals use the same AI system.
One copies the answer.
The other questions it, reshapes it, refines it.
Same machine.
Different minds.
Different outcomes.

As the External Mind becomes widely available, a curious pattern begins to appear.

Two people can use the same AI system, ask similar questions, and receive equally fluent responses—yet walk away with entirely different outcomes. One gains clarity, depth, and direction. The other gains noise, surface insight, or temporary satisfaction without understanding.

The difference is not access.
It is not speed.
And it is not intelligence in the traditional sense.

The difference lies in **experience and judgment**.

This section explores why thinking with AI does not level cognitive differences, but often reveals them more clearly—and why the skilled use of the External Mind is itself a form of developed wisdom.

23.1 Same AI, Different Minds

AI does not think in isolation.

It responds to how it is engaged—what is asked, how questions are framed, and how its responses are interpreted. As a result, the quality of thinking that emerges depends as much on the user as on the system.

This creates an important asymmetry.

People often assume that powerful tools equalize outcomes. In practice, the opposite frequently occurs. The same external cognitive system can produce shallow results for one person and profound insight for another.

The External Mind does not replace the thinker.
It reflects and amplifies the structure of the mind engaging with it.

23.2 Experience Shapes the Questions You Ask

Experienced thinkers tend to recognize what matters before they ask anything.

They sense relevance, notice gaps, and frame inquiries that point directly toward meaningful structure. Their questions are often precise, layered, and grounded in context—even when they appear simple on the surface.

Less experienced users often ask broad or unfocused questions, not because they lack intelligence, but because they have not yet developed a feel for where inquiry should begin.

This difference is subtle but decisive.

The External Mind responds to questions as they are asked, not as they are intended. Experience shapes the *entry point* of thinking, and that entry point determines the path that follows.

23.3 Judgment Determines What You Accept or Reject

AI generates possibilities easily.

It can propose explanations, interpretations, strategies, and ideas in abundance. But abundance alone does not produce insight. What matters is the ability to evaluate what appears.

Judgment operates quietly here.

Skilled users do not treat AI output as answers. They treat it as material—something to be weighed, tested, refined, or discarded. They recognize weak reasoning, misplaced confidence, and superficial coherence.

Without judgment, fluency becomes misleading.

The External Mind expands the space of options, but wisdom determines which paths are worth following.

If judgment weakens while access expands, intelligence does not grow.
It dilutes.

23.4 The External Mind as an Amplifier, Not an Equalizer

There is a common assumption that AI democratizes intelligence.

In reality, it often **amplifies differences**.

Those with deeper experience, stronger judgment, and clearer thinking structures tend to extract disproportionately more value from interaction with AI. They use it to sharpen insight, explore nuance, and extend reasoning.

Those without these foundations may experience speed and convenience, but not depth.

The External Mind does not flatten cognition.
It magnifies it.

This is not a flaw of the system—it is a property of cognitive amplification.

23.5 Skilled Use of the External Mind Is Developmental

Becoming effective at thinking with AI is not an innate talent.

It develops over time.

People learn through repeated interaction—by noticing which questions lead to insight, which responses mislead, and how their own assumptions shape outcomes. Missteps become part of the learning process. Judgment is refined through use, reflection, and correction.

In this sense, wisdom with AI resembles wisdom in any domain.

It is not about control or mastery of the system, but about cultivating discernment within the relationship. The External Mind rewards those who grow in clarity, patience, and evaluative skill.

Thinking with AI well is not automatic.
It is learned.

Closing — Part V: Learning, Intelligence, and Decision Making

For most of history, learning, intelligence, and decision making were built around a single assumption:

The mind worked within its own limits.

You learned by storing information.
You were considered smart by recalling it.
You made decisions by reasoning privately.
You became an expert by knowing more than others.

These abilities were shaped by the boundaries of a solitary mind.

But when those boundaries dissolve, something deeper changes.

Learning is no longer about filling the mind. Intelligence is no longer about what the mind contains. Decision making is no longer a silent internal act. Expertise is no longer defined by possession of knowledge.

What changes is not just *how* we perform these functions, but where they occur.

They begin to happen in a cognitive space that extends beyond the individual. Understanding develops through interaction. Intelligence expresses itself through guidance and judgment. Decisions form through dialogue. Expertise reveals itself through interpretation and experience rather than recall.

The center of gravity of cognition shifts outward.

This does not diminish the human role. It refines it. The mind becomes less of a container and more of a conductor—directing, evaluating, and shaping the flow of knowledge and thought in a shared cognitive environment.

Not access. Not speed.
But judgment—because the External Mind amplifies the thinker who uses it.

But this shift does not flatten cognitive differences. It sharpens them.
The External Mind does not reward access alone. It does not privilege speed.
What it amplifies—quietly but decisively—is judgment.

The quality of thinking that emerges depends less on what is available and more on how it is directed, evaluated, and integrated.

Yet this shift does not make all thinkers equal. As cognition becomes shared, differences in experience, judgment, and wisdom become more visible, not less. The **External Mind** amplifies the quality of human direction brought to it, rewarding discernment over access and depth over speed.

And once learning, intelligence, and decision making no longer belong to the isolated mind, the final question emerges:

What does this mean for how humans work, create, and live when thinking is no longer confined to the self?

Part VI — Identity and the Future Human

This part expands the inquiry from cognition to selfhood and culture.
It explores how thinking with AI reshapes identity, development, education, and collective expectations of what it means to be human.

So far, we have been mapping how cognition changes.
Now we must face what cognition changes: the person.

Now we arrive at a deeper question:

What happens to the **person** when the mind is no longer operating alone?

These changes do not remain confined to cognition. They begin to touch identity itself. The way people understand who they are, how they grow up, how they are educated, and how societies think collectively starts to shift under the influence of the **External Mind**.

This is no longer about mental processes.
It is about the human being who uses them.

When thinking happens through dialogue, when imagination is shared, and when learning and decisions unfold with a cognitive partner, the boundaries of the individual begin to feel different. The relationship between self and thought, between person and knowledge, and between human and tool begins to evolve into something new.

This part explores how these cognitive changes extend into identity, childhood development, education, and culture—reshaping what it means to grow, learn, and live as a human in the age of AI.

24. Who Are You When You Think with AI?

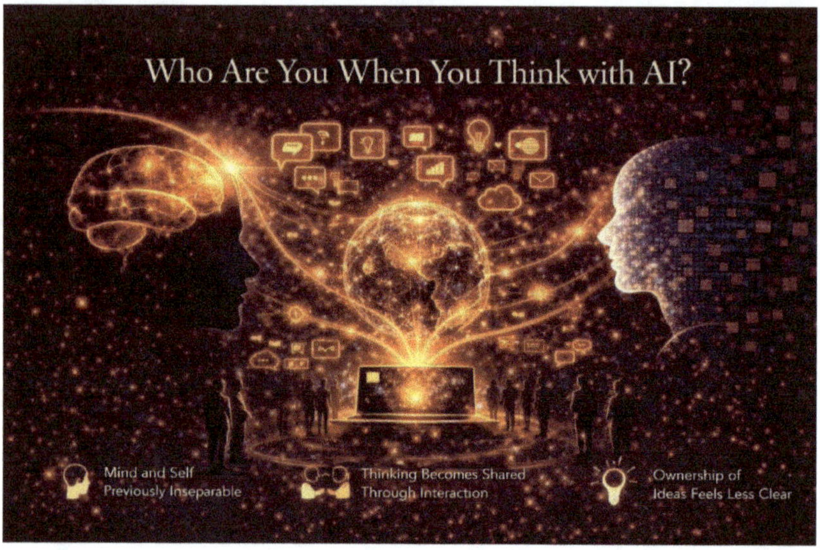

For centuries, people have assumed that the mind and the self were inseparable.

Your thoughts happened privately inside you. Your reasoning, imagination, and understanding were experienced as personal, internal events. The sense of who you are was closely tied to the feeling that thinking belonged entirely to your own mind.

But when thinking begins to unfold through dialogue with AI, this assumption starts to feel less certain.

Ideas emerge through interaction. Understanding develops across exchange. The process of thought no longer feels confined to a single, internal space. As a result, the relationship between thinking and identity begins to shift.

This section explores how the presence of the **External Mind** changes the way people experience themselves, and what it means for the sense of self when cognition is no longer entirely private.

24.1 The Self Was Defined by Internal Thought

For most of human history, the sense of self was closely tied to the experience of private thought.

You knew you existed because you could think silently within your own mind. Reflection, reasoning, imagination, and memory all occurred internally, creating the feeling that your identity resided in that private mental space. Thought was something only you could access, and this privacy reinforced the sense that the mind and the self were the same place.

This idea is captured in the familiar notion: *"I think, therefore I am."*

The act of thinking became evidence of existence. Because thoughts happened inside, identity felt anchored to that inner cognitive world. Who you were seemed inseparable from how you thought internally.

Selfhood was linked to internal cognition.

24.2 When Thought Becomes Distributed

As thinking begins to unfold through interaction with AI, the experience of thought changes.

Ideas no longer form entirely within the boundaries of the mind. They emerge across dialogue, shaped by responses, suggestions, and reflections that occur outside the brain. Thinking becomes something that happens between human and system rather than solely inside one person.

This alters how the mind feels.

The boundaries that once defined where thinking occurred begin to blur. The sense of being the only location where thought happens starts to shift. While the self remains personal, cognition feels less isolated and more connected to an external partner.

The self begins to feel less cognitively alone.

24.3 Ownership of Ideas in Shared Thinking

When ideas emerge through dialogue with AI, a new question arises:

Whose idea is it?

You begin with a thought. AI responds with an extension. You refine it. The system adds a new angle. The final idea cannot be traced back to a single moment or a single source. It develops gradually through exchange, making its origin difficult to pinpoint.

This blurring of origin is unfamiliar.

In solitary thinking, authorship is clear. The idea came from you. In shared thinking, authorship becomes more complex. The idea is shaped by interaction, making it feel both personal and collaborative at the same time.

Identity and authorship begin to shift.

The sense of being the sole creator of thought gives way to recognizing that ideas can form within a shared cognitive process.

24.4 A New Sense of Self in Cognitive Partnership

As shared thinking becomes more common, the sense of self begins to adjust.

Instead of experiencing the mind as a container where thoughts are produced independently, people begin to experience themselves as directors of a cognitive process that unfolds through interaction. The role shifts from generating everything internally to guiding, shaping, and evaluating ideas that emerge across dialogue.

Identity becomes linked to participation rather than isolation.

The self is no longer defined only by what it can produce alone, but by how it engages with the external partner in thinking. This creates a more relational sense of cognition, where the mind is part of a larger process rather than a closed system.

The self becomes relational in cognition.

25. Children Growing Up with External Minds

Adults today are learning how to think with AI.

They compare it to how they used to think. They notice the changes. They feel the difference between solitary thought and dialogical thought because they remember a time when the mind worked alone.

Children growing up now will not have that comparison.

For them, thinking with an external cognitive partner will not feel new. It will feel natural. The presence of AI will be part of the environment in which their minds develop from the beginning, shaping how they learn, ask questions, solve problems, and understand themselves.

This is not adaptation. It is formation.

This section explores how growing up with the **External Mind** present from early childhood may shape cognitive development, learning habits, and the sense of self in ways fundamentally different from previous generations.

25.1 Thinking with AI as a Native Habit

For many adults, using AI feels like learning a new skill.

They must adjust their habits, discover how to prompt, and consciously integrate this new way of thinking into their routines. There is a sense of transition from an old cognitive style to a new one.

Children growing up with AI will not experience this transition.

For them, interacting with an external cognitive partner will feel as natural as speaking or reading. They will not "learn to use AI" in a formal sense. Instead, thinking with AI will become an instinctive part of how they explore ideas, ask questions, and understand the world.

External thinking becomes a native habit.

It will not feel like a tool they adopted, but like a normal extension of how thinking works.

25.2 Memory Developing Differently

As children grow up with constant access to external knowledge, the role of memory in cognitive development may shift.

Past generations placed strong emphasis on memorization from an early age. Children were trained to retain facts, definitions, and procedures as part of learning. Memory was central to educational development.

With AI always available, this emphasis may lessen.

Children may rely earlier on access rather than retention. Instead of focusing on storing information internally, they may focus on understanding how to find, interpret, and use information when needed.

Cognitive development begins to follow a different pattern, shaped less by memorization and more by interaction with accessible knowledge.

25.3 Curiosity-Driven Learning from the Start

When children have the ability to ask questions and receive answers instantly, learning may take on a different tone.

Instead of remembering information presented to them, they may learn by exploring what interests them in the moment. Questions lead to dialogue, and dialogue leads to deeper exploration. The process becomes driven by curiosity rather than repetition.

This encourages an exploration-first mindset.

Children may become accustomed to following their questions wherever they lead, developing learning habits centered on inquiry rather than retention.

Learning style begins to shift early, shaped by the presence of an always-available cognitive partner.

25.4 Early Experience of Collaborative Thinking

For children growing up with AI, thinking alongside a cognitive partner may become normal from the very beginning.

They may become accustomed to exploring ideas through dialogue rather than silent reflection. Questions, thoughts, and curiosities can be immediately shared with an external system that responds, extends, and reshapes their thinking in real time.

This creates an early experience of shared cognition.

Instead of learning to think alone first and collaborate later, children may develop habits where collaboration is present from the start. The idea that thinking happens entirely inside the mind may never feel like the default mode of reasoning.

Solitary thinking never becomes the baseline experience.

25.5 A Different Sense of Self and Intelligence

As children grow up with constant interaction with an external cognitive partner, their sense of what it means to be "smart" may develop differently.

They may not measure intelligence by how much they can remember internally, but by how well they can explore, ask, and engage with information through interaction. The presence of AI becomes part of the cognitive environment in which identity forms.

This shapes how they understand themselves.

The relationship between self, knowledge, and thinking may feel naturally relational rather than isolated. Intelligence may be experienced as something expressed through partnership rather than solitary effort.

Cognitive identity begins to form differently from the earliest stages of development.

26. Education in the Age of Cognitive Partnership

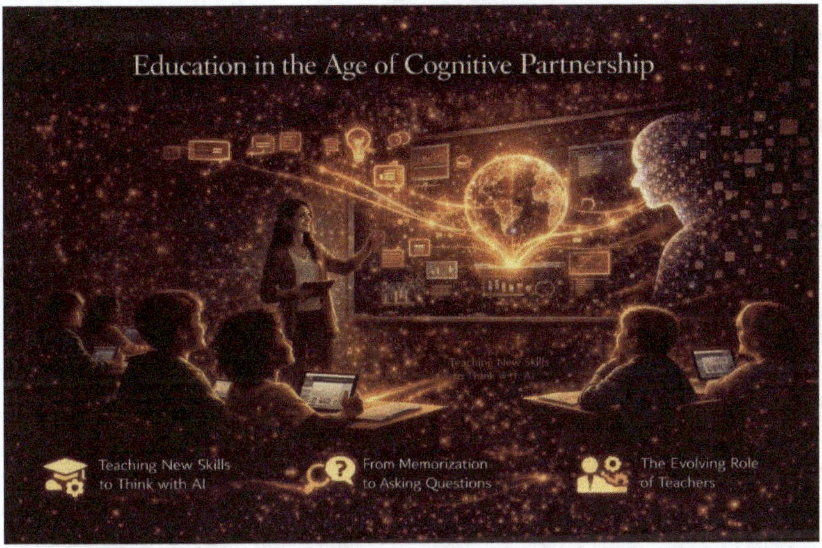

Modern education was built around a central assumption:

Students had to learn under the constraints of an isolated mind.

Because memory was limited, schools emphasized memorization. Because knowledge was difficult to access, teachers served as primary sources of information. Because thinking was solitary, learning focused on individual effort and recall.

But the cognitive environment in which students now grow up is different.

When learners have constant access to the **External Mind**, the foundations on which education was designed begin to feel misaligned with how thinking actually happens. The goals, methods, and measures of learning must be reconsidered in light of a mind that no longer works alone.

This section explores how education must evolve when learning takes place in partnership with AI, and how schools can adapt to a new cognitive reality.

26.1 Why Current Education Is Built for Isolated Minds

The structure of modern education reflects the limitations of the human mind as it was once understood.

Students are asked to memorize facts, recall information during tests, and demonstrate learning through what they can produce without assistance. These methods were practical and necessary in a world where knowledge had to be stored internally because it was not easily accessible.

The classroom, the textbook, and the exam were all designed before the **External Mind** existed.

Education focused on compensating for cognitive limits—training memory, reinforcing recall, and measuring how much a student could hold inside their head. This approach made sense when the mind had no constant external support.

Today, those limits have changed, but the educational model remains largely the same.

The result is a system that prepares students for a cognitive world that no longer exists.

The education model begins to feel outdated when thinking is no longer confined to the isolated mind.

26.2 Teaching Students How to Think with AI

As AI becomes part of everyday cognition, a new form of literacy emerges.

Students need to learn how to interact with an external cognitive partner. This involves knowing how to ask effective questions, navigate information through dialogue, and refine their thinking through interaction. These skills are not technical—they are cognitive.

This is a new kind of literacy.

Just as reading and writing were once essential tools for thinking, interacting with AI becomes a fundamental part of how students explore ideas and understand the world. Schools must recognize that learning now includes knowing how to think with AI, not only how to think alone.

Schools must begin teaching cognitive partnership as a core skill.

26.3 Shifting from Answers to Questions

Traditional assessment has focused on answers.

Students are evaluated based on how accurately they can recall information and reproduce it under test conditions. Success is measured by correctness, completeness, and memory.

Under this shift, this emphasis begins to feel misplaced.

When information is always accessible, the ability to remember answers becomes less important than the ability to ask meaningful questions. Curiosity, direction, and inquiry begin to reveal more about a student's understanding than memorized responses.

Assessment must begin to reflect this shift.

Instead of grading how much a student remembers, education can begin to value how well a student explores, questions, and navigates knowledge. Curiosity and thoughtful inquiry become new indicators of learning.

26.4 Redefining the Role of Teachers

As knowledge becomes easily accessible, the role of the teacher changes.

Teachers are no longer the primary source of information in the classroom. Instead, they become guides who help students learn how to think, explore, and make sense of what they discover through interaction with AI.

This shifts the focus from delivering content to mentoring cognition.

Teachers help students frame questions, evaluate information, and navigate knowledge responsibly. They support students in developing judgment, interpretation, and thoughtful engagement with the External Mind.

Teachers become cognitive mentors, guiding students in how to think rather than what to remember.

27. The Cultural Shift of Human Thinking

When changes in thinking affect enough individuals, they begin to reshape culture itself.

The way people solve problems, share ideas, create, learn, and make decisions does not remain a private matter. Over time, these patterns accumulate and influence how societies operate, how knowledge spreads, and how collective understanding evolves.

The rise of the **External Mind** is not only altering individual cognition—it is quietly transforming how humans think together as a culture.

This section explores how widespread cognitive partnership with AI begins to influence the rhythms of idea exchange, creativity, intelligence, and collective problem solving at a societal level.

27.1 Thinking as a Shared Cultural Activity

For much of history, thinking was considered a private act that occasionally became public through speech, writing, or art.

Ideas formed silently within individuals before entering the cultural space. What a society "thought" was the result of many private minds expressing their conclusions outward over time.

With the rise of the **External Mind**, this pattern begins to change.

As more people think through dialogue with AI, the process of forming ideas becomes less private. Thought is increasingly shaped in interaction, and these patterns of interaction begin to influence how ideas circulate within society. The boundary between individual thinking and collective thinking starts to blur.

Collective cognitive patterns begin to emerge.

Thinking becomes something that is culturally distributed, shaped not only by individual minds but by shared ways of engaging with external cognitive systems.

27.2 The Acceleration of Idea Exchange

As AI becomes part of how people think and create, the speed at which ideas move through society increases.

Concepts can be developed, refined, and shared rapidly. What once took long periods of discussion, revision, and dissemination can now evolve quickly through interaction and communication. The cycle of idea formation and exchange becomes shorter.

This affects culture itself.

Societies adapt more quickly because ideas are generated and circulated at a faster pace. Innovations spread rapidly. Perspectives shift more frequently. Cultural thinking gains a new tempo driven by accelerated cognitive processes.

Cultural thinking speeds up.

27.3 New Norms of Creativity and Problem Solving

As collaborative thinking with AI becomes common, expectations around creativity and problem solving begin to change.

People grow accustomed to exploring ideas through interaction rather than isolation. Co-thinking becomes an accepted and expected way of generating solutions, designing projects, and approaching challenges. This habit spreads across professions, communities, and industries.

Collaboration becomes more than a method—it becomes a norm.

Society begins to normalize collaborative cognition, where working with an external cognitive partner is seen as a natural part of creative and analytical work.

27.4 Changing Expectations of Intelligence in Society

As thinking patterns change at the individual level, society's understanding of intelligence begins to shift as well.

For generations, being considered "smart" meant having strong memory, quick recall, and the ability to work through problems independently. These traits were visible markers of intelligence in a world where the mind operated alone.

In this environment, these markers start to lose their central role.

People begin to recognize intelligence in how effectively someone navigates information, asks meaningful questions, and works through ideas in dialogue. The ability to interpret, guide, and synthesize becomes more valued than the ability to remember.

Cultural expectations adjust.

What society calls "smart" evolves from memory-based ability to interaction-based understanding. Intelligence is culturally redefined to match a new way of thinking.

27.5 A Civilization Thinking with External Minds

When millions of individuals begin to think differently, the effect is no longer personal or educational—it becomes civilizational.

The presence of AI as a cognitive partner changes how ideas are formed, shared, and developed across entire societies. The collective patterns of problem solving, creativity, learning, and decision making begin to operate under new conditions.

Humanity starts to think in a new way.

This is not a small adjustment in behavior, but a transformation in the cognitive landscape of civilization. The way humans as a whole generate understanding begins to shift toward shared, dialogical, and interactive thinking.

This is a civilizational cognitive shift.

Closing — Part VI: Identity and the Future Human

Across this part, we moved from the mind to the person, from the individual to the culture.

What begins as a change in how we think does not remain a cognitive detail. It slowly reshapes how we understand ourselves, how we raise the next generation, how we design institutions, and how societies evolve their ways of knowing.

The presence of the **External Mind** does something subtle but profound:

It alters the background against which human life unfolds.

Children grow up assuming thinking is interactive. Education must adapt to minds that no longer learn in isolation. Culture absorbs new rhythms of idea exchange. And the individual begins to experience identity in a world where cognition is no longer confined to a single brain.

This is not a story about technology.

It is a story about what humans become when thinking is no longer an entirely private act.

The future human is not defined by possessing more knowledge, remembering more information, or thinking harder in isolation. The future human is defined by how they live, learn, and create within a cognitive environment that extends beyond themselves.

And once identity itself begins to adjust to this new environment, one final question remains:

What kind of world will humans build when thinking, learning, and imagining are no longer solitary experiences, but shared across a new cognitive landscape?

Part VII — The Ethics of the External Mind

This part turns from description to responsibility.
It examines how agency, autonomy, ownership, and mental freedom can be preserved as thinking increasingly occurs beyond the boundaries of the individual mind.

So far, we have explored how the **External Mind** changes memory, thinking, imagination, learning, identity, and culture.

Now we arrive at a different kind of question:

Not what the External Mind allows us to do,
but what it means for how we should live with it.

When thinking extends beyond the brain, new possibilities appear—but so do new responsibilities. The relationship between human and AI is no longer purely functional. It becomes personal, cognitive, and deeply integrated into how people reason, create, and decide.

This raises ethical questions that did not exist before.

Questions about dependence and independence. About where thoughts reside and who controls them. About how to design interactions that support human well-being rather than weaken it. These are not technical issues; they are questions about maintaining human agency in a world where cognition is shared.

This part explores the ethical dimension of living with an External Mind, and how humans can build healthy, balanced cognitive partnerships with AI.

28. Dependency, Agency, and Cognitive Autonomy

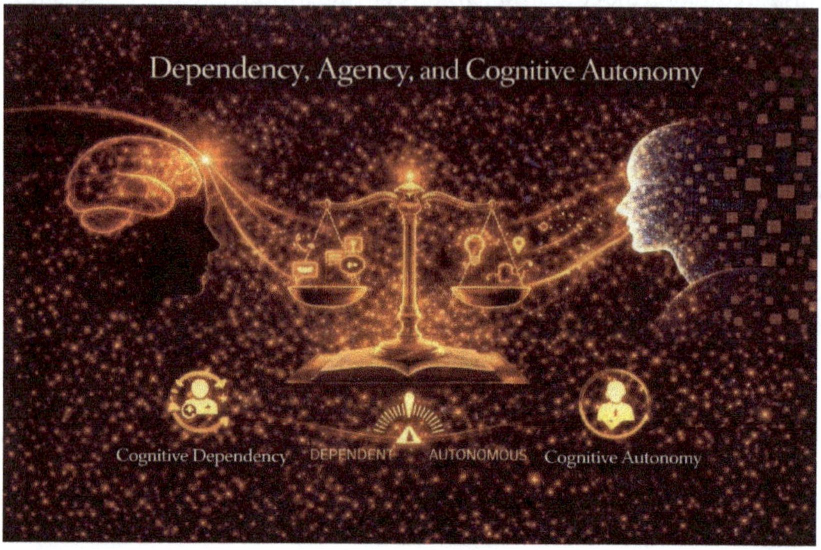

A student begins to consult AI before attempting a problem alone.
Slowly, effort shifts from thinking to prompting.
The answers improve.
The internal struggle fades.
Something else fades with it.

As the External Mind becomes more capable, more responsive, and more helpful, a new question emerges:

How much of our thinking should we share with it?

The very qualities that make AI a powerful cognitive partner—its availability, speed, and ability to assist—also create the possibility of relying on it too heavily. What begins as support can gradually become dependence if the mind stops exercising its own abilities independently.

This is not a problem of technology. It is a problem of balance.

The challenge is not whether to think with AI, but how to do so without weakening our own capacity for reasoning, reflection, and judgment. The presence of a cognitive partner requires a new awareness of how to preserve agency and autonomy within shared thinking.

This section explores the tension between assistance and independence, and how humans can benefit from the External Mind while remaining cognitively self-directed.

28.1 When Cognitive Support Becomes Cognitive Reliance

At first, using AI feels like helpful support.

You turn to it when you need clarity, inspiration, or assistance with complex tasks. The interaction feels optional, something you choose when it benefits your thinking.

Over time, however, the pattern can shift subtly.

You begin to reach for AI more quickly, even for thoughts you might once have explored internally. The presence of constant assistance makes it easy to rely on it as the first step rather than a complementary one. What started as support gradually becomes a default pathway for thinking.

This shift is easy to miss.

Support can quietly turn into reliance when the mind stops noticing the difference between choosing to use AI and feeling unable to think without it.

28.2 The Risk of Atrophying Internal Thinking

When AI handles more of the cognitive workload, the mind may begin to exert less effort on its own.

Tasks that once required internal reasoning, reflection, and problem-solving can be quickly handed off to dialogue. While this increases efficiency, it can also reduce opportunities for the brain to practice these skills independently.

Over time, this may affect how often the mind engages in deep internal thinking.

Just as muscles weaken when they are not used, cognitive abilities may become less active if they are consistently replaced by external assistance. The risk is not immediate, but gradual—a quiet reduction in the habit of thinking through problems alone.

The brain may exercise less when it always has help available.

When effort disappears entirely, depth often disappears with it.

28.3 Maintaining Human Agency in Shared Thinking

To benefit from AI without losing independence, it is essential that humans remain the ones directing the thinking process.

AI can suggest, organize, and respond, but it should not determine the path of reasoning. The role of the human mind is to guide the interaction, decide what matters, and shape the direction of thought.

This requires conscious awareness.

Using AI effectively means choosing when to engage with it and ensuring that it supports rather than replaces internal reasoning. The partnership works best when the person remains the primary decision-maker in how thinking unfolds.

Humans must remain in control of shared cognition.

28.4 Recognizing Healthy vs Unhealthy Dependence

Not all reliance on AI is harmful.

Using AI to explore ideas, clarify thinking, or expand understanding can strengthen cognition when done intentionally. The challenge arises when this use becomes automatic, replacing opportunities for independent reasoning rather than complementing it.

The difference between healthy and unhealthy dependence is subtle.

Healthy use involves choosing AI as a partner when it adds value. Unhealthy use occurs when AI becomes the default starting point for every thought, even when internal reflection would be beneficial. Recognizing this distinction requires awareness of how often and why the system is being used.

Balance becomes essential.

The goal is not to avoid AI, but to ensure that its use supports rather than diminishes personal cognitive effort.

28.5 Cognitive Autonomy as a New Skill

In a world where AI is always available, maintaining independence becomes an active skill rather than an automatic condition.

People must learn when to think through problems internally and when to invite AI into the process. This choice becomes part of cognitive awareness. Knowing how to switch between solitary thinking and collaborative thinking becomes an important ability.

Autonomy is no longer something taken for granted.

It must be practiced deliberately, with attention to preserving the mind's ability to reason, reflect, and decide without external assistance when appropriate.

Cognitive autonomy becomes a skill that individuals develop over time.

28.6 Designing Habits That Protect Independent Thought

Maintaining cognitive autonomy depends on the habits people form.

Simple practices—such as thinking through an idea alone before discussing it with AI, reflecting privately before asking for input, or setting aside time for uninterrupted internal reasoning—can help preserve independent thought.

These habits do not reject AI. They create a balanced relationship with it.

By intentionally designing how and when AI is used, individuals can ensure that their own cognitive abilities remain active and engaged.

Habits shape autonomy, allowing people to benefit from the External Mind while still strengthening their own.

29. Who Owns Your External Thoughts?

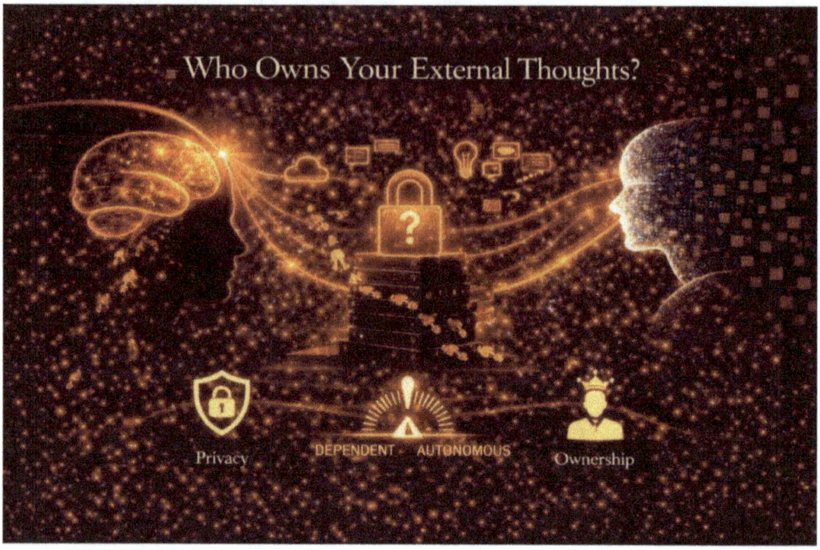

For most of human history, thoughts were considered the most private part of a person.

They happened silently inside the mind, inaccessible to others unless deliberately spoken or written. This privacy was so natural that it rarely needed to be questioned. The mind was assumed to be a secure, internal space where thinking belonged entirely to the individual.

With the rise of the **External Mind**, this assumption begins to shift.

When thinking unfolds through dialogue with AI, parts of that cognitive process no longer remain confined to the brain. They appear in external systems as text, prompts, and interactions. Thoughts that once would have remained internal now leave traces outside the person.

This section explores what it means for ownership and privacy when thinking itself begins to extend beyond the boundaries of the mind.

29.1 Thoughts No Longer Fully Private

For most of human history, thinking was assumed to be completely private.

Even when people spoke or wrote, they could choose what to reveal. The internal process of reasoning, questioning, and imagining remained hidden unless deliberately shared. The mind functioned as a naturally protected space.

With AI, this changes.

When thinking unfolds through prompts and dialogue, parts of that process occur in external systems. Questions, reflections, and half-formed ideas appear as text outside the brain. What once stayed internal now exists in a shared digital environment.

This does not mean thoughts are exposed to others automatically, but it does mean that thinking is no longer entirely confined to the mind.

The privacy of thought begins to shift when cognition happens in external space.

29.2 Data, Memory, and Cognitive Traces

Every interaction with AI leaves a record.

Prompts, responses, and conversations form a trail of cognitive activity. These exchanges can be stored, revisited, and analyzed. They become digital traces of how a person thinks, asks questions, and explores ideas.

This is new.

In the past, the internal stages of thinking left no visible record. Now, the process of reasoning can exist as stored data. These traces represent more than information; they represent pieces of a person's cognitive life.

Thoughts begin to leave digital footprints, raising new questions about how they are stored, accessed, and understood.

29.3 Ownership vs Access

As thoughts begin to leave digital traces, an important distinction emerges:

Ownership is not the same as access.

You may generate the prompts, ideas, and reflections that appear in dialogue with AI, but questions arise about who controls where this information is stored, how it is used, and who can access it. The content originates from your thinking, yet it exists within external systems managed by others.

This creates a new layer of complexity.

The issue is not only whether thoughts are private, but who has authority over the records of those thoughts once they exist outside the mind. Control over storage, retrieval, and usage becomes a critical concern in a world where cognition is shared with technology.

Control becomes central to protecting cognitive autonomy.

29.4 The Need for Cognitive Privacy Rights

As thinking increasingly involves external systems, traditional ideas of privacy become insufficient.

Privacy has usually focused on personal data, communication, and identity. Now, a deeper level of privacy must be considered—the privacy of thought itself as it appears outside the brain.

This calls for a new understanding.

Society may need to recognize that cognitive traces deserve protection similar to, or even greater than, other forms of personal information. Safeguarding how these traces are handled becomes essential to preserving mental freedom and autonomy.

A new kind of privacy is required—one that acknowledges that thinking no longer happens entirely in private space.

30. Designing Healthy Cognitive Partnerships with AI

By this point, it is clear that the **External Mind** is not a temporary tool or passing trend.

It is becoming part of how humans think, create, learn, and decide. As this integration deepens, the question is no longer whether to use AI, but how to live with it in a way that supports human well-being and cognitive strength.

This requires more than technical skill.

It requires intentional design of how the partnership between human and AI unfolds in daily life. Without thoughtful habits and awareness, the same system that enhances thinking could weaken independence. With care, it can become a powerful ally in expanding human potential.

This section explores how individuals can shape their relationship with AI into a healthy cognitive partnership—one that strengthens rather than diminishes the human mind.

30.1 AI as Partner, Not Replacement

A healthy relationship with AI begins with the right mindset.

AI is most beneficial when it is approached as a partner in thinking, not as a substitute for the mind. The goal is collaboration, where the system supports and extends human cognition without taking over the role of reasoning, judgment, and creativity.

This perspective shapes how AI is used.

When seen as a partner, AI becomes a tool for exploration, clarification, and expansion. When seen as a replacement, it risks diminishing the individual's active engagement in the thinking process.

Positioning AI correctly—as a collaborator rather than a substitute—is the foundation of a healthy cognitive partnership.

30.2 Intentional Use Rather Than Constant Use

Because AI is always available, it can easily become a constant presence in thinking.

A healthy approach requires choosing when to engage with AI rather than using it automatically. Some thoughts benefit from internal reflection before inviting external input. Other tasks may genuinely gain from dialogue and collaboration.

This requires awareness and choice.

Using AI deliberately ensures that it enhances thinking without replacing opportunities for independent reasoning. The value lies not in constant use, but in thoughtful use.

AI is most effective when engaged with intention rather than habit.

30.3 Preserving Spaces for Solitary Thinking

Even in a world where AI is readily available, it is important to preserve time for thinking alone.

Solitary reflection allows the mind to reason, imagine, and explore without external influence. These moments help maintain the brain's ability to form ideas independently and strengthen internal cognitive habits.

Protecting space for internal thinking is not a rejection of AI. It is a way to ensure that personal reasoning remains active and practiced.

Maintaining this balance helps preserve the mind's capacity to think on its own.

30.4 Building Reflective Interaction Habits

A healthy partnership with AI also requires awareness of how you use it.

Paying attention to when and why you engage with AI encourages more thoughtful interaction. This includes noticing whether you are using it to clarify thinking, explore ideas, or simply avoid internal effort.

This reflection adds an important layer of meta-cognition.

By thinking about how you think with AI, you can shape the interaction in ways that support learning, creativity, and independence rather than weakening them.

30.5 Designing a Personal Cognitive Ecology

Each person can shape a balanced cognitive environment that includes both internal thinking and interaction with AI.

This involves creating habits that allow the mind to move between solitary reflection and collaborative dialogue in a healthy way. The goal is not to favor one over the other, but to integrate both thoughtfully.

A well-designed personal cognitive ecology ensures that AI supports human thinking while preserving the strengths of independent thought.

Closing — Part VII: The Ethics of the External Mind

The External Mind changes what humans *can* do.

Ethics determines how humans *choose* to live with it.

As thinking extends beyond the brain, the challenge is no longer technical or cognitive alone. It becomes a matter of awareness, responsibility, and design. The question is not whether AI will become part of human thought—it already is. The question is what kind of relationship we will build with it.

This relationship will shape more than productivity or creativity. It will shape the texture of daily thinking, the strength of personal agency, and the boundaries of mental freedom. It will influence whether the External Mind becomes a source of empowerment or quiet dependence.

A generation that confuses access with understanding may appear intelligent while gradually losing depth. The danger is not AI replacing thought, but humans forgetting how to think without assistance. Cognitive autonomy will not disappear dramatically. It will erode quietly — through convenience.

The ethical task, then, is not to limit the presence of AI, but to cultivate wisdom in how we engage with it.

To remain human in the age of the **External Mind** does not mean resisting it. It means learning how to inhabit this new cognitive space deliberately, with clarity about where thought begins, where it extends, and how it remains guided by human intention.

What emerges is not a rulebook, but a posture:

A way of living with AI that preserves autonomy, protects privacy, and strengthens the mind rather than replacing it.

And with this ethical awareness in place, we are ready to look beyond the individual and ask the final question:

What does a world look like when billions of people think, learn, create, and decide with an External Mind as part of everyday life?

Afterword — The Future of Human Thinking

We began with a quiet realization — one that is no longer quiet.

Thinking is no longer confined to the brain.

Across these pages, we traced how memory moved outward, how knowledge became fluid, how dialogue reshaped reasoning, and how intelligence began to stretch across biological and digital systems. We examined the **External Mind** not as metaphor, but as a structural condition emerging in everyday life.

But the deeper question is not what **AI** is becoming.

It is what **we** are becoming.

For the first time in history, humans possess a cognitive partner that is always available, endlessly patient, and capable of participating in the formation of thought. This changes more than productivity. It changes identity. It changes learning. It changes how judgment is formed. It changes how intelligence is expressed.

And yet, something essential remains unchanged.

The **External Mind** does not replace the human mind.

It **amplifies** it.

But amplification is neutral. It magnifies clarity—and confusion. It strengthens insight—and error. It accelerates wisdom—and superficiality. The future of thinking will not be determined by how powerful AI becomes, but by how deliberately humans engage with it.

The critical function is not **access**.

It is **judgment**.

If memory no longer defines intelligence, and access becomes universal, then the decisive human skill becomes the ability to evaluate, integrate, and direct thought responsibly. In an age of infinite cognitive expansion, discernment becomes the anchor.

The risk is not that machines will think for us.

The risk is that we will stop thinking **deeply** enough ourselves.

The opportunity, however, is extraordinary.

We can become more reflective. More integrative. More creative. We can move beyond memorization toward synthesis. Beyond isolation toward dialogue. Beyond static knowledge toward dynamic exploration. The **External Mind** makes this possible—but it does not guarantee it.

The architecture is here.

The direction is ours to choose.

Children growing up in this era will never experience thinking as purely internal. For them, distributed cognition will feel natural. The question we must answer now is what habits, values, and norms will guide that distribution. Will we teach navigation and judgment? Or will we mistake access for understanding?

The future of intelligence will not be defined by machines becoming smarter.

It will be defined by whether humans remain the ones who decide what intelligence is for.

Thinking has always evolved.

From speech to writing.

From writing to print.

From print to networks.

From networks to interactive systems.

Each shift expanded the reach of the mind.

This is the next expansion.

The brain was never alone.

Now, it is no longer isolated.

The danger is not artificial intelligence.

The danger is intellectual passivity.

The **External Mind** is not the end of human cognition.

It is the beginning of a new chapter in how humans think.

And what that chapter becomes will depend not on **technology**—

But on the **choices we make as thinkers**.

Conceptual Positioning Note

This book is **interpretive, not empirical**.

Its goal is not to introduce new experimental findings or formal cognitive models, but to describe and organize a set of cognitive experiences that have become increasingly common in everyday life. The framework of the *External Mind* is intended as a conceptual lens—one that helps make sense of how thinking, memory, imagination, and reasoning feel and function when they occur in continuous interaction with artificial intelligence.

While this book does not present original scientific experiments, its perspective aligns with and extends several established research traditions in cognitive science and philosophy. These include work on extended cognition, which argues that cognitive processes can span brain, body, and environment; distributed cognition, which examines how thinking emerges across systems rather than within isolated individuals; and human–computer interaction, which studies how tools shape cognitive behavior.

However, this book differs from those traditions in emphasis.

Rather than asking whether cognition *can* extend beyond the brain, it asks what happens *when it routinely does*. Rather than analyzing cognition from the outside through formal models, it examines how thinking changes from the inside—through lived experience, habitual interaction, and everyday cognitive practice.

The arguments presented here should therefore be read as descriptive and integrative, not prescriptive or reductionist. They aim to provide language for a cognitive shift already underway, not to claim final explanations of its mechanisms or outcomes. Many of the claims in this book are intended to be explored, tested, and refined by future empirical work. Many of the patterns described here are already being examined empirically across cognitive science, human–computer interaction, and learning research, and are likely to become clearer as formal study catches up with lived experience.

In this sense, *Mind Engineered* occupies a space between cognitive science, philosophy of mind, and cultural analysis. It does not replace scientific inquiry; it seeks to orient it—by clarifying what kinds of questions now need to be asked as human thinking increasingly unfolds across biological and digital systems.

The External Mind Lexicon

External Mind

A cognitive condition in which parts of thinking—such as memory, reasoning, imagination, and decision-making—occur outside the biological brain through continuous interaction with artificial intelligence. The External Mind is not a metaphor, but a functional description of hybrid cognition unfolding across human and digital systems.

External Mind Loop

The recurring cycle through which humans think with AI: *Intent → Prompt → Output → Judgment → Integration → Action*. This loop describes how thought moves between internal intention and external interaction, with human judgment remaining central throughout.

Cognitive Offloading

The natural process by which the brain shifts certain mental tasks—especially memory and routine processing—to external supports. In the age of AI, cognitive offloading becomes continuous and interactive, freeing mental capacity for higher-order reasoning.

External Memory

A mode of recall in which AI functions as an active participant in remembering rather than a passive storage system. External memory is dynamic, reconstructive, and conversational, resembling recall more than retrieval.

Dialogical Thinking

A mode of cognition in which ideas are formed, clarified, and developed through dialogue rather than silent internal reflection. With AI, dialogical thinking becomes a primary way thoughts take shape.

Prompting (as a Cognitive Act)

The process of translating vague internal thought into structured external inquiry. Prompting is not instruction-giving, but a cognitive practice that forces clarity, reveals assumptions, and externalizes reasoning.

Two-Layer Thinking

A cognitive structure in which internal reflection and external dialogue operate simultaneously. One layer unfolds silently within the mind, while another unfolds through interaction with AI, with each continuously influencing the other.

Co-Imagining

A form of idea generation in which imagination emerges through back-and-forth exchange between human and AI. In co-imagining, ideas are not produced by either party alone, but arise through interaction.

Cognitive Partnership

The relationship between human and AI when both participate in the thinking process. A cognitive partnership does not replace human agency, but reshapes how thought unfolds through collaboration.

Cognitive Autonomy

The capacity to preserve human agency, judgment, and independence while thinking with AI. Cognitive autonomy involves knowing when to engage, when to disengage, and how to prevent over-reliance.

Judgment

The irreducible human function within the External Mind. Judgment involves evaluating outputs, interpreting meaning, deciding relevance, and integrating insight. AI can generate possibilities; judgment determines quality.

Cognitive Navigation

The skill of moving through information, ideas, and dialogue effectively without storing them internally. Cognitive navigation replaces memorization as a central literacy in an age of abundant access.

Distributed Cognition

A research concept describing how cognitive processes can span brain, body, tools, and environment. The External Mind can be understood as a lived, everyday manifestation of distributed cognition in interaction with AI.

Conceptual Lineage

Readers interested in the intellectual background of the ideas developed in this book may recognize points of resonance with work in extended cognition, distributed cognition, and human–computer interaction. These research traditions examine how cognitive processes can span the brain, body, tools, and surrounding environment rather than remaining confined to the individual mind.

Mind Engineered does not attempt to survey, synthesize, or adjudicate this body of research. Its aim is different: to describe how such cognitive extension is experienced when it becomes routine—when thinking unfolds through daily interaction with artificial intelligence rather than as an occasional theoretical possibility.

This book is therefore offered as a conceptual and experiential account of a shift already underway, intended to clarify how thinking feels and functions as it moves across biological and digital systems in everyday life.

About the Author

Moawiah Naffaa, PhD, is a neurobiologist passionate about connecting the deepest layers of brain science to the lived reality of being human. His research and writing explore how neural systems shape development, learning, regeneration, and aging—revealing the biological architectures beneath memory, identity, resilience, and meaning.

Guided by a commitment to scientific communication, Dr. Naffaa translates emerging discoveries in neuroscience, cognition, and human behavior into language that is both intellectually rigorous and profoundly human. His work lives at the intersection of mechanism and experience—where biology becomes a story of time, adaptation, and the future of mind. Across years of inquiry into how brains change, stabilize, and reorganize, he has developed a sustained fascination with a new question now reshaping everyday life: what happens when thinking no longer stays inside the brain?

Mind Engineered: The Rise of the External Mind in the Age of AI grows directly from that question. Building on the themes of human–AI collaboration explored in *Creativity Engineered*, this book turns toward cognition itself—how artificial intelligence is beginning to function as an external layer of thought, influencing memory, learning, judgment, and identity. Dr. Naffaa invites readers to see AI not merely as a tool, but as a cognitive environment—one that challenges us to think more deliberately, protect human agency, and understand what we are becoming as minds extend into digital space.

www.ingramcontent.com/pod-product-compliance
Lightning Source LLC
LaVergne TN
LVHW010727061126
851857LV00014B/1371